"Dr. Carol is uniquely qualified to a[...] complicated relationship between ou[...]. In *Sexpectations*, she draws upon her professional expertise as both an ob-gyn and an ordained minister to examine this relationship with compassionate wisdom. Her redemptive perspective offers hope and help for those who live with the dissonance of a sexual story that feels out of alignment with their faith. I highly recommend this book for its informed and practical approach to mapping a path forward whereby those stories can be redeemed."

Bill Buker, DMin, PhD, LPC, associate dean and senior advisor to the university on wellness; senior professor of counseling, Graduate School of Theology and Ministry, Oral Roberts University

"As a pastor I see the struggle so many people experience around sexual issues. There's such a need, both in the church and in the world, to show people a path to sexual wholeness that is both compassionate and truth-filled. Dr. Carol's new book is full of grace and truth—just like Jesus was. She shows readers how to bring Jesus into their sexual story so they can be whole in their hearts and know what God has next for them, married or single."

Joe Champion, senior pastor, Celebration Church, Georgetown, Texas; author, *Confronting Compromise*

"We all have a sexual story that contains chapters of brokenness, confusion, and mismanagement. Dr. Carol does a masterful job of inviting the reader to explore their story in a hopeful and redemptive way. She offers a competence and compassion for those eager to write new chapters to their sexual story."

Jonathan Daugherty, founder and president, Be Broken Ministries

"Dr. Tanksley presents a beautifully rich and gentle resource for men and women alike to reframe sex, sexuality, and relationships. A thought-provoking read that isn't afraid to dive into hard places while exploring the whole of our sexual story and inviting the grace of Jesus to transform and heal."

"As someone who has sexual trauma in her past and experiences same-sex attractions, it was refreshing to read a book that includes my type of sexual story—not as a footnote, but simply as another version of sexual brokenness that must be tenderly examined alongside everyone else's story. This book paves a gospel-hopeful path forward, no matter our sexual history."

"Dr. Carol is your friend through this entire book. Like a caring big sister, she asks powerful questions in a way that unravels shame and self-hatred—exposing the enemy and creating space for the real and personal Jesus to put His gentle finger on 'that' place and say, 'Here, let's deal with this.' Dr. Carol is a credible, compassionate, fun, and understanding guide, helping you on a safe path to courageously go where you have never gone to receive what you were designed to have: true intimacy and Jesus! This book is an essential resource for every pastor and counselor. I am excited to share this with our Love Triumphs community of women; this book will accelerate so much healing and sexual wholeness."

"*Sexpectations* is a must-read addition to ongoing conversations about godly sexuality. Author Carol Tanksley delves into what about our story keeps us from embracing God's design for sex and how we can pursue sexual wholeness and intimacy. Couples, singles, pastors, and counselors should add this book to their shelves!"

"Most of us carry a tremendous amount of unaddressed expectations when it comes to sex and sexuality in our lives. In this honest and thoughtful book, Dr. Carol helps us unpack the baggage we carry around and learn to live with compassion toward our own story. This book addresses many of the conversations we all wish we could have in a safe, Christ-centered manner. I believe you will find this book just as helpful and meaningful as I did."

Nick Stumbo, executive director, Pure Desire Ministries

"A home run! Dr. Carol Tanksley writes with wisdom, experience, compassion, and biblical understanding, gently inviting you to take a deep dive into sexual wholeness and true intimacy. Sidestepping superficial strategies, she invites you to ask tough questions and bravely confront the issues keeping you imprisoned, and offers fresh insight pointing to freedom and wholeness. A marvelous work."

Gary Thomas, author, *Sacred Marriage* and *Cherish*

"Feelings surrounding sex, intimacy, and love can cloud our actions and desires—they can hinder our love relationships. These emotions need to be tackled to have victory in our love life with people and with God. Dr. Carol will guide you as you unpack any hindrances connected to intimacy and direct you into wholeness, into fullness, into a life where you can thrive. *Sexpectations* is a brilliant work and one I highly recommend."

Lucille Williams, women's director; author, *The Intimacy You Crave: Straight Talk about Sex and Pancakes*

"Dr. Carol Tanksley has created a path of healing in the pages ahead. Her readers will find hope and restoration as she shares from her experience in helping hundreds heal from their sexual past. Dr. Tanskley does an incredible job of reminding us that we are not called to shame, but called to Jesus as our ultimate healer. This is a book that will help you and help you help others!"

Jonathan Pokluda, lead pastor, Harris Creek Baptist Church; bestselling author; podcast host, *Becoming Something*

sexpectations

sexpectations

reframing your good and not-so-good
stories about God, love,
and relationships

Carol Tanksley, MD, DMin

Chosen

a division of Baker Publishing Group
Minneapolis, Minnesota

Published by Chosen Books
Minneapolis, Minnesota
ChosenBooks.com

Chosen Books is a division of
Baker Publishing Group, Grand Rapids, Michigan

Printed in the United States of America

Library of Congress Cataloging-in-Publication Data
Names: Peters-Tanksley, Carol, author.
Title: Sexpectations : reframing your good and not-so-good stories about god, love, and relationships / Carol Tanksley MD, DMin.
Description: Minneapolis, Minnesota : Chosen Books, a division of Baker Publishing Group, [2024] | Includes bibliographical references.
Identifiers: LCCN 2023035089 | ISBN 9780800763497 (trade paper) | ISBN 9780800772741 (casebound) | ISBN 9781493442386 (ebook)
Subjects: LCSH: Sex—Religious aspects.
Classification: LCC BL65.S4 P48 2024 | DDC 241/.664—dc23/eng/20230922
LC record available at https://lccn.loc.gov/2023035089

The examples in this book are fictional composites based on the author's experience talking and corresponding with hundreds of patients, clients, and website visitors over many years. All names are invented, and any resemblance between these accounts and actual persons is coincidental.

Author is represented by the literary agency of Credo Communications, LLC, www.credocommunications.net.

Baker Publishing Group publications use paper produced from sustainable forestry practices and post-consumer waste whenever possible.

24   25   26   27   28   29   30   7   6   5   4   3   2   1

To Al,
for being the person with whom I could
experience the intimacy I didn't know was possible.
You were, are, and always will be
the wind beneath my wings.
I love and miss you, honey!

contents

introduction

I found myself alone. In a hotel room. With a married man.

His opening prayer said one thing, but his hands and his attempt at a kiss made abundantly clear the real reason he was there.

But why was I there? I knew better. I was doing exactly what I had said I would never do and until then had not done. The occasional "professional" meetings with this man over the past couple months could have predicted this moment. The way my body and brain had responded to his hugs at those meetings could have predicted it too. Why had I continued to seek his advice? Why had I said yes to his request to come up to my hotel room to "pray"?

The prospect of marriage seemed long gone to my never-married fortysomething self. As my body responded to his touch, a half-formed thought flashed through my mind: *Would this be my best and perhaps last chance to experience something I want? Could this be as good as it gets for me?*

Sex. It's everywhere. Love it or hate it, it affects you deeply. Few if any areas of human experience carry more weight.

On one hand are those who would say, "It's just sex." They make it sound like your sexual desires hold no more meaning than your hunger for food. The animals do it, people do it. It's natural. What's the big deal?

On the other hand, there are those who would say something like, "Just say no. Until your wedding night. Then once you say 'I do,' say yes." You're supposed to turn off your sexuality until one specific moment, then turn it on. (And has that led to *happily ever after*?)

Why is your heart not satisfied with either of those narratives? Even if your head buys into one of them you can't shake the feeling that something is missing. Neither of those messages seems adequate for your story.

Perhaps porn is a part of your life. It has been for a long time. If sex is just sex, why does the porn leave you feeling dirty? Why do your prayers for God to take away your desire for porn never seem to work? Doesn't He care? You're burning up inside. What more are you supposed to do?

Or perhaps you hate sex. Most of the time even the idea of sex makes you cringe inside. But you're married, so you're not supposed to hate it. You're supposed to not deprive your spouse of their "conjugal rights." That's what you've been told the Bible says. You wonder if you're a complete failure as a spouse and a Christian. Maybe you can shut down your body and mind and just do it, but that makes your spouse even more upset.

Maybe you want sex, your spouse doesn't, and you feel cheated.

And then you might be a single person. You were married, and then your spouse passed away, or you're divorced. Or you've had plenty of sex but not with a spouse, perhaps before becoming a Christian and now you're trying to figure things out. Friends with benefits, or living with a boyfriend/girlfriend. You've had sex, and you like it. But something inside you isn't at peace about this sex thing. You can't quite live with the "It's just sex" idea. But you feel like you need sex, and you're not getting it from a spouse, so what are you supposed to do? Is your disquiet simply an echo of those who have tried to legislate morality? You're certainly not buying into that, at least not anymore.

Perhaps you're sexually attracted to someone of the same sex, and the clash between what culture says and how the Christian church has traditionally responded leaves you unsettled. Maybe you can't shake the horrible feeling that no one, including God, will ever want you if they really knew what you've done. You find it maddening that you can't let go of the sexual stuff that happened to you a long time ago.

Or perhaps you find yourself alone in a hotel room with a married man.

The ideal story often told—boy meets girl, they fall in love, have wonderful sex for the first time on their wedding night and live happily ever after—is not your story. All the lists about what is sin and what isn't haven't helped you. (By the way, what's actually on the sin list? And who gets to make up the sin list, anyway?) All the discussions of Bible verses about marriage and sex haven't helped much. If you pray, all the begging and pleading with God to fix you hasn't helped. Perhaps you've given up on praying.

What's wrong? Why does a "simple" biological function mess with your head so much?

The answer I would propose is that for humans, sex is anything but a simple biological function. It's much more than a behavior. Trying to handle issues around sex and sexuality from a primarily behavioral standpoint is deeply unsatisfying. And it just doesn't work.

Sex Is about Matters of the Heart

That's what this book is about: matters of the heart around sex and sexuality.

It's not a biblical defense of classical Christian teaching on sexuality, though we'll talk about the Bible. You won't find an outline of what sexual behaviors are sin or not sin, though we won't be afraid to talk about sin. You won't find an endorsement of or polemic against the purity culture that some in the church grew up in a few decades ago, though purity (a word not easily defined) has some benefits. You won't find tips and tricks that will guarantee fireworks-glorious sex with your spouse, though your married sex life may well get better.

What you will find is a pathway to dealing with your sexual story.

Yes, you have a sexual story. Some of that story may be good, even very good. But if "good" described your whole sexual story you wouldn't be reading this book. There's part of your sexual story that's not so good. You've "crossed the line" somewhere, and it's weighing on you. Your old mental tapes or painful memories won't leave you alone. There might be some truly ugly parts of your sexual story, unspeakable things that happened to you, that you've engaged in, or that you've done to yourself or others. Yup, we're going there.

We're going to talk about the chapters in your story that brought you to where you are now. Nothing is too small, too gross, or too dark. Knowing the truth—including the truth of your sexual story—will set you free.

We're going to invite Jesus into your sexual story. You know He already knows your story, but what about inviting Him right into the middle of it? And actually letting Him in? Nothing stays the same when Jesus shows up. Your sexual story won't stay the same when He shows up there, either.

And then we're going to write a new chapter. You will be the author, or more correctly the coauthor of the next chapter of your story, your sexual story. You'll see how your transformation is not primarily something God does *for* you, but it's something He and you work out *together*. Married or unmarried, young or old, with few regrets or too ashamed to even think about it, you and God together will write that new chapter.

As an ob-gyn physician for thirty years, I've helped many women deal with the most intimate aspects of their bodies, lives, and relationships. As an ordained Christian minister and personal coach, I've helped thousands of women, men, and couples find the transformation God has for them in the deepest parts of their souls. Every single day I hear from people all around the world, men and women, from age twelve to eighty-two, in every conceivable relationship status, who are desperate for that transformation in their sex lives. And I've seen their heartache, trauma, and shame *healed*.

You, too, can experience the transformation God has for you, in a deeper way than you've yet imagined. I believe that because I've seen people experience it. And I believe it because I've experienced it myself. I'm not "done." No one is. The transformation God offers is a process. A process that leads to wholeness, integration, and living fully alive.

In that hotel room I heard myself say words that came from somewhere beyond me: "I can't do this." My clothes did not come off. Miraculously, he left.

But my inner world was rocked. It was time to deal with my sexpectations—all the marred and distorted messages I had come to believe, the wounds I had accumulated, and the empty places in my own soul. There was a lot of junk to deal with and a lot of new things to learn.

As I did that work, my story lost its sting. And as part of the next chapter of my story, I once again found myself alone in a hotel room with a married man. But this time I was a married woman, and the married man was my husband! My wedding night was wonderful, but only because I had dealt with the matters in my own heart. I was privileged to experience a happy, loving, sexually intimate marriage during the years Al and I were together prior to his death in 2016.

Your story can lose its sting too. I don't know what the next chapter of your story will be or whether you will experience a sexually satisfying marriage or not, but I do know that you can become sexually whole. You can experience huge dimensions of sexual wholeness here and now, even while we all await the ultimate intimacy we will experience in eternity.

So let's explore God's answer to your sexual story. The next chapter could be much better than you ever imagined.

how could this happen?

Whoever drinks of the water that I will give him will never be thirsty again.

Jesus

Alice heard the doctor's words, and it felt like a death sentence: "It's herpes." She had a seminary degree, a leadership role in her church, and an AARP card, but never a wedding ring. Now she also carried an STD. How could this happen? Oh, Alice knew the biology of how herpes happens. But how could this happen to *her*? When she called me that morning, her voice was confused— not about herpes, but about how she could end up in a place she had determined she would never go. She loved God and was following Him. The decades of wanting to be married and never quite getting to "I do" had been wearing on her. Ending up in bed with her on-again, off-again boyfriend felt unstoppable at the time. But a short time later, in the doctor's office and then getting that fateful call, her life felt like it came to a full stop.

Charles was new to this Christianity thing. He'd been quite the sex magnet during his teens and early twenties and slept with just about anyone he wanted to. Last year God disrupted him and captured his heart; glory! Then somehow, he got the message that following Jesus would mean something different for his sex life—was it something someone said, or was it the Spirit's work in his heart? It seemed hard to figure this all out. Larissa, Charles's new Christian girlfriend, wanted to talk about what limits, if any, they should put on their physical relationship. The idea of not having sex had never occurred to him. Would she leave him when she learned about his sexual past? He was glad Jesus had forgiven his sins, but his past and his attraction to Larissa were making things seem complicated.

Brianna had wanted to do everything right, and she thought she had. Her prayers for a godly husband seemed to be answered. She was a virgin on her wedding day, and Marty was too. They had met at a Christian college and were excited about going into ministry together after graduation. But if she did everything right, why did Marty's kiss after their "I do" at the altar make her body cringe? And why did her stomach revolt each time he told her how good she was at sex? Intercourse kept getting increasingly painful even though her doctor said there was nothing physically wrong. The messages she'd heard about marriage and married sex didn't seem anything like real life. Brianna began to seriously wish there would be a morning when she wouldn't wake up.

Love it or hate it, sex is a big deal.

Love it or hate it, sex is a big deal.

You likely know it's a big deal; you also know it's complicated. At first, porn wasn't a big deal. You certainly didn't wake up one morning and decide to get hooked on porn and thereby mess up your life, future marriage, and relationship with God. You didn't intend to cause your spouse pain by closing off your body and soul. You didn't plan to get an STD or have multiple abortions or sexually violate or betray your spouse.

Perhaps you've awakened to what feels like your sorry state and decided you want things to be different. It may not be easy, but you're determined to change. So you gather all the inner gumption you've got and you draw a line in the sand. *Just do it!*

You're going to stop watching porn, so you delete your browser history on your phone and computer so porn doesn't pop up as easily, and vow to stop using private browsing. You know your spouse will want sex tonight so you brace yourself and determine to say yes. Or you tell your "friend with benefits" that there will be no more benefits.

And maybe that works for a while. For a few days or several weeks, no more porn. You power through having sex with your spouse a few times. Friday night finds you somewhere else instead of in someone else's bed. You can do this!

But a few days, a few weeks, or even a few months later, things fall apart. You're on a business trip, tired and frustrated, and the porn channel is only one click away. Or the torrent of resentment and pain flowing out of your soul becomes deafening and you push your spouse away. (Note: Saying no to your spouse's request for sex is not sin. Please keep reading.) Or one night, with nothing better to do, you text so-and-so, they answer, one thing leads to another, and . . .

You feel guilty. Like a failure. You're ashamed of yourself for being so weak. You've got to just try harder. *I know, I need to pray. God will help me. That's what I've been missing.*

So you ask for God's forgiveness, hoping you haven't gone too far already. It's hard to believe He isn't mad at you, but you use all the mental strength you've got to choose to believe He does forgive. Maybe you get on your face and ugly-cry, repenting and pleading and begging for His help to change.

Please take away my desire for porn.

Make me want to have sex with my spouse.

Forgive me this time and I'll never sleep around again.

And you go back to white-knuckling it. It works—for a few days, or a few weeks, or even a few months. Until it doesn't. The pressure becomes too great and you mess up again. And the shame cycle becomes deeper while self-loathing messages scream in your head. You're on a binge-purge cycle that you can't seem to stop. God doesn't seem to be doing anything to help.

No, you didn't choose to have sexual issues. But as someone once poignantly told me, "Now my issues have issues."

You might have listened to sermons and read a bunch of books. You might have asked others to pray for you or stepped up your own prayer life. You might have come to the point where you've decided it's too hard. Christianity's "sex is for marriage" message is outdated, and you've let the cultural flow of "anything goes" carry you along. (How's that working out for you?)

> Dealing with your sexual issues requires looking at your sexual story with both honesty and compassion.

But here's the game-changing reality: Addressing sexual issues from a right-or-wrong behavioral standpoint is like treating a life-threatening abscess with Tylenol and a Band-Aid. Your fever might go down and you might feel a little better temporarily, but it can still kill you. The only way to solve your issues is to get under the surface and deal with the roots of what's going on.

Pulling off the bandage and lancing the abscess will hurt, but that hurt has a purpose and won't last forever. The process of dealing with your sexual issues requires looking at your sexual story with both honesty and compassion—the way Jesus looks at your story.

I love how Jesus is revealed in John 4. During His travels He stops to rest at a community well outside a Samaritan city. A woman comes to draw water, and Jesus involves her in conversation. She's thirsty, and Jesus offers her living water.

"That sounds great! Let me have some of this living water."

"Go call your husband," Jesus responds.

"I don't have a husband."

"You're right; you don't have a husband. You've had five, and the man you're with now is not your husband."[1]

And just minutes later the woman goes running back into town telling everyone she meets, "This man told me everything I ever did."

Jesus did not magically make a movie of her whole life pass before her eyes. She felt like He did because He put his finger on the *core issues* in her heart. Interpretations of this story often assume the woman was sexually promiscuous. She might have been, but that's not the only possible interpretation. In those days life expectancy was much shorter—perhaps her husbands had died from disease or through fighting in a war. Divorce was not uncommon; perhaps her husbands had put her away. Regardless of why she had had five husbands, Jesus was not condemning her. He was saying, "I see you. This is where you're stuck. Come, let's deal with this. I'm a safe place for you to deal with your issues." Jesus was looking at her with both honesty and compassion, and inviting her to look at her own story the same way.

That's what Jesus is inviting you to do too—look at your sexual story with both honesty and compassion. That's the way to disinfect the shame, find healing, and truly change your heart so you can write a new chapter going forward. This new chapter is one where you not only behave differently, but you *are* different, on

23

the inside. It will empower you to grow in lasting sexual whole-ness and pursue the kind of intimacy your heart desires and that God desires for you.

Whatever you did or whatever was done to you in the past can lose its sting. Your soul can become satisfied, connected, and whole. That's the future God has for you.

That's where we're going. Let's begin the task of looking at your sexual story.

Where Sexual Issues Come From

What words or phrases describe how you feel about sex and sexu-ality? Pause and notice what's going on in your heart right now. What feelings are coming up even as you are reading this? You might feel:

- Frustrated
- Desperate, needy
- Ashamed, guilty
- Confused
- Tired, overwhelmed
- Revulsion
- Hurt, betrayal
- Pleasure, desire
- Invaded, vulnerable
- Dirty
- Anxious, afraid
- Ambivalent (love it, hate it)
- Excited, because it's taboo

Those are some of the ways the men and women who took the *Sex*pectations course we offer online (which established much of the framework for this book) said they felt about sex and sexuality. If you needed evidence that sex is about more than biology and physical acts, look at this list and at the emotional angst stirring in your own soul right now. How your heart responds to this topic is an important clue to what's under the surface.

Remember, if powering through and trying harder worked, you wouldn't be here. The angst you're carrying is itself a reason to look further.

So where does that ambivalence, desperation, pain, fear, or frustration around sex come from? Issues always come from somewhere. Where did yours begin? A helpful way to consider that question is to ask yourself how you were sexually formed.

> **You were sexually formed long before you realized what was happening.**

You were sexually formed long before you realized what was happening. By "sexually formed," I'm talking about something much deeper than a discussion about biology, birds, and bees. You are a sexual being whether you are having sex or not, and regardless of how you feel about sex. God created you that way. You may or may not be thrilled at that thought, but it's part of who you are.

The way you came to be who you are sexually is not simple. Seminary professors Judith and Jack Balswick write, "Human sexuality does not arrive fully formed, but rather develops as an interactional process."[2] Genetics, hormones and other biological factors, family behavioral patterns, cultural norms, specific teaching (from school, church, etc.), personal experiences, and more all play a role.

While researchers can generalize and describe common ways people develop, your own story is unique. No one else has your exact biological makeup, family history, and life experience.

Remember, you didn't wake up one day and decide to have issues. Unpacking how you were sexually formed goes a long way in getting to the roots of your issues. This is not a blame-and-shame game. It's looking at your story with honesty and compassion, the way Jesus does. As you read the following paragraphs, be aware of any feelings of self-contempt or shame that may try to distract your attention. If so, know that you can't eliminate shame by just trying not to feel ashamed, but you can notice the temperature in your inner world and choose to keep going anyway. Put your inner critic on time-out for a little while.

You absorbed things from your environment growing up. Even as an infant and young child you picked up attitudes about relationships, intimacy, and sexuality from others. Consider a few of the earliest elements of your sexual formation:

- Was being born a girl or a boy good news to your parents? Or was one of them (or both) hoping for a child of the other gender?
- As you became aware of your body, especially your sex organs, what messages did your parents or caretakers provide? How was your curiosity handled? Were you shamed?
- What did you observe about how your parents or caretakers expressed intimacy? How did they "do" feelings and communicate? What subtext did you pick up about sex?
- How did you first learn about sex itself? What feelings accompanied those first learning moments? Desire?

Anxiety? Curiosity? Shame? All of the above, or maybe something else?

Did answering these questions reveal any attitudes and feelings about your earliest beliefs around sex and sexuality? It is rarely obvious; it takes pondering. Even very observant parents often miss clues about when their child is internalizing and processing messages about sex and gender. Many people with sexual issues have a certain ambivalence around sex that is evident early on. You may be aware of whether you mostly love sex or mostly hate it, but know this: It is a complex area of human experience and complex feelings are normal. You would be unusual indeed if you had a perfect environment in which to process your earliest feelings, questions, or understandings around sex. And if your family was dysfunctional, welcome to the club! (Where are the truly functional families anyway?)

Those earliest experiences "taught" you things that may not have seemed directly related to sex, but they play a big role in your sexuality today. Consider these elements:

- Is the world a mostly "safe" place where my needs are generally met? Or is the world a place where I can expect only harm? Is the world mostly dog-eat-dog, survival-of-the-fittest, where I must claw and grasp for my needs to be met?
- What do I do when I feel bad? Do I feel competent to manage my internal environment? Do I ignore it? Fall apart? Demand or wait for others to "fix" me?
- What role do other people play in my life? Am I often a "victim" in relation to others? Do I sometimes exploit and

27

manipulate others to get what I want? Is true give-and-take possible?

- How do men and women relate to each other? Are men generally weak or angry or exploitative? Are women generally needy or manipulative or there to be used?

Perhaps you can see how sex is not just about sex. Your angst around sexuality is connected to all these other elements of your human formation.

Marty "learned" that men are generally weak, and that negative feelings were to be stuffed. Watching porn made him feel momentarily powerful. It became his default way of soothing himself when he felt anxious or inadequate. Marrying Brianna, he expected to get that same feeling of being powerful from having sex with her. But the only way to capture that feeling was to exploit, demean, and act out on her the destructive things he had seen portrayed in porn.

Every human being—including you—has in some way been harmed sexually.

Marty didn't wake up one day and decide to mess up his marriage by abusing his wife sexually. His early exposure to porn wasn't his choice, but it harmed him sexually. For Marty to deal with his sexual story will require facing a lot of shame.

Brianna learned about sex not from her mother, but from a girl at school a couple years older than her. Sex seemed both scary and exciting. Somewhere along the way, she picked up the message that a good Christian wife always gives sex to her husband. "The Bible says so." And she dutifully complied. Marty's distorted sexual appetite was just something she would have to put up with. *A good Christian wife doesn't say no*, she thought. The message of "a Christian wife must always give her husband sex" became part of how she was harmed sexually.

Charles had a hard time remembering a time he didn't know about sex; it was part of the world he lived in. He saw the normalization of almost every kind of sexual behavior in music, social media, and even school. It was, well, normal. He would have never considered it harmful. But now that he's wrestling with what following Jesus means for his sex life, it's raising new questions.

Distorted sexual beliefs may be one factor leading to sexual issues, but there are many ways you may have experienced sexual harm. Dr. Dan Allender, Christian therapist, author, and professor, implores us to recognize how prevalent this is.

> For many, this means giving up the presumption that we have not suffered sexual harm. We all have. Each and every individual on the earth has known some assault against their gender and/ or their genitalia. Some of the harm is obvious and severe. Other harm is so subtle and normalized that it seems ridiculous to call it abuse. But sexual abuse is often far subtler and extensive than most of us have considered.[3]

It is especially painful to explore the parts of your sexual story where you have been harmed sexually. Some categories of sexual harm, as Dr. Allender expresses, are more obvious. Your grandfather sexually molested you when you were five. You were date-raped as a freshman in college. Your priest or your older brother showed you porn and manipulated you into acting it out. Your stepfather sold you to his friends for sex. If you experienced such horrendous harm, I pause to grieve with you.

But maybe you were never molested or raped, and you're wondering how you could have been harmed sexually.

Remember that you learned about sex, about life, about relationships before you realized you were learning. Perhaps you observed your father while drunk (or not drunk) drag your mother into the bedroom. Or your mother had a steady string of boyfriends churning through the house. Or one of your parents had an affair, or made snide (or subtle) remarks about the other's sexuality. Imagine some other child or adolescent living in the home you grew up in. What would they have come to believe about sex, relationships, and intimacy? Those distorted messages create templates in your mind that you cannot easily or quickly override simply by wanting to think differently. That's sexual harm.

You might have been sexualized much too soon. While there's much to celebrate in dance, beauty pageants, acting, or similar experiences for young people, our culture is so sexualized that for many children and adolescents, such activities become a gateway for sexual harm. Your value can become equated with your sex appeal. It takes a vigilant parent to nurture the positive aspects of those environments while also jealously protecting you from sexual harm. I question whether it's even possible to fully protect a child who is immersed in such an environment.

Try putting "God" and "sex" in the same sentence. What emotional tone would that sentence have?

For all the progress society has made in making sexual abuse more okay to talk about, covert sexual damage is not often addressed. When a parent's marriage is unhealthy, it's very easy for one parent to look to a child to meet some needs that should legitimately only be met by a spouse. As a child, you're put in the impossible position of having to meet intimacy needs for a parent such as emotional support, hearing about sexual struggles, or keeping secrets. Such unhealthy dynamics damage your ability to develop healthy intimacy on your own in the future. It's a form of sexual harm.

Sexual harm, whether overt or insidious, leaves deep marks on your soul that play out in your sexual behavior. The beliefs you've come to hold and your (perhaps unseen) wounds are framed by what happened to you. And we haven't yet spoken of the spiritual aspects of how you were sexually formed.

Consider these questions:

- How does God feel about sex? Does He see it primarily as a "necessary evil" in order to keep the human species going?
- How did you learn about how God feels about sex? Who told you God feels that way?
- Are these messages different from what you've heard in church about sex? If so, how?
- How does God feel about *you* and sex? Does He leave the room when you have sex? Is He demanding you behave in a certain way sexually? Would He prefer you turn off your sexuality?

You probably wouldn't be reading this if you believed God and sex had nothing to do with each other. Evaluating how you were formed sexually includes examining the verbal and nonverbal religious messages that have attached to sex in your mind, and how that happened.

Try putting "God" and "sex" in the same sentence. What emotional tone would that sentence have? For many Christians, it would have a sense of shame. God's out to curb your pleasure. He's watching for you to mess up, and if He catches you, look out. He'll find a way to punish you. You've got to try harder to get it together if you want to be close to Him. Or perhaps your thought process would be more like, *God wants me to be happy, so He's okay with whatever sexual stuff makes me happy.*

Thankfully there are fewer shame-based messages in the church today than there were years ago. But even today most of the sex talk in Christian circles is about what is or is not on the sin list. It's all focused on behavior.

Just yesterday I talked with twenty-two-year-old Stephanie. Breaking up with her boyfriend felt traumatic. They never had intercourse, but "We were both trying to get as close to the line as we could. I shouldn't have let things get that far." Shame and heartbreak are mixed together in her soul. Maintaining different physical boundaries might have left Stephanie feeling less bad about herself afterward. But where did that shame come from?

Stephanie learned about sex from the cold and distant relationship between her parents, and from watching countless hours of porn. All she heard at church about sex was, "Sex is only for marriage." It's not hard to imagine how those elements of her sexual formation left Stephanie confused—not intellectually, she believes she knows what's right. She wants to be married, but she has no mental templates of a healthy intimate relationship between a husband and wife that would help her imagine a healthy future for herself. She's had no wise and safe place to address her own sexual desires or her struggle with porn.

Religious messages have been part of your sexual formation too. Some might identify that as the problem: Just strip sexuality of any religious baggage and you'll be fine. Sex is just sex. But we're contending that sex is never just sex. It can't be. In the next couple chapters, we'll address the spiritual implications and meaning around sex more deeply.

For now, let's continue to contemplate how you were formed sexually, how you came to feel as you do and believe what you believe around matters of sex.

Examining Your Sexual Story

Looking at your sexual story with both honesty and compassion can seem daunting. Honesty? You may have invested considerable emotional energy in trying to dismiss or ignore particular elements of your story that tend to make yourself or others look bad. It seems easier to hide. Humans have had lots of practice hiding, ever since the garden of Eden. *Let's pretend that didn't happen.*

And compassion? In some ways that's even more daunting than honesty. Self-contempt seems more natural, or even godly. In some way we all move toward self-contempt. You believe the lie that if you weren't worthy of contempt, you wouldn't have experienced the sexual harm that you did. You should have said no, or known better, or not let that happen, or not let it affect you, or responded differently. It seems easier to shoulder the load of blame yourself than to experience the vulnerability of being harmed, lied to, or used.

And then what about what you did in response? The lies you "chose" to believe, the hookups you engaged in, the porn you watched, how you responded or didn't respond to your spouse sexually, the lines you crossed, the vows you broke, the people you used sexually and harmed along the way. Compassion? That seems impossible.

But pause for a moment. What if you imagine the younger you as someone else? It's time to embrace that compassion for yourself.

Did that six-year-old child even know what porn was? Did that fourteen-year-old adolescent have a clue what her sexual exploration would lead to? Did that nineteen-year-old college student really understand the consequences of his sexual behaviors? Did that young married wife really have the option to say no? Did that young couple know the first thing about building a healthy intimate relationship?

Compassion doesn't excuse bad behavior, but it's a critical piece in the journey toward sexual wholeness. And it's the basis of the invitation Jesus is offering you.

Your sexual story hasn't happened in a vacuum. Your story is part of a much larger story, one that's full of romance, betrayal, intrigue, rescue, and happily ever after. We're about to look more at that larger story of which you're a part, and how your individual story fits in.

In this book we'll talk a lot about inviting Jesus into your sexual story. For right now, let's start by visualizing a starting point.

MEETING HIM

With some time on your hands one weekend afternoon, you decide to maybe catch a movie or get a cup of coffee. Ambling through the parking lot, you notice a group of people making a bit of a ruckus. They all seem to be gathered around a central figure. Your steps turn that direction. Could this be Him? There's been a lot of buzz among your coworkers and friends, buzz about Him. Your curiosity has been aroused, but the stories you've heard seem like fantasy, too good to be true. But if the stories you've heard are even partly true, about what He's done for others, could there be a crumb of it for you? You've tried and hoped before and always ended up disappointed. Yet it feels like something invisible is drawing you.

Maybe you'll hang around the edge of the group and just watch. You try to catch some of the words. The long-disappointed flicker of hope in your heart feels awakened. But you remind yourself that you've been down this road before; you better leave before your hopes get dashed once again.

You're about to turn away when He sees you.

Oh, the look in His eyes. In that moment you forget about the movie and the coffee. You lose sight of the people around. It's as if you and He are the only two people in the universe. You've never seen eyes like His. He really sees you. All of you. He sees more of you than you want anyone to see. But instead of feeling rejected, you feel drawn. His eyes hold you. Maybe the goodness in His eyes is what is pulling you toward Him, keeping you from leaving. Your nervous system seems about to blow a fuse. And then He speaks: "I'm coming to your house."

My house? Can't be. Surely He was speaking to someone else. But He was looking right at me. He saw me. Me!

Your brain needs time to process what's happened. What next? My house? When? Now?[4]

Questions to Discuss or Contemplate

- What about your sexual story prompted you to pick up this book?
- How were you sexually formed? Look over the questions throughout this chapter and discuss or write about the important parts of your sexual formation.
- How have you been sexually harmed?
- What feeling do you experience as you contemplate Jesus seeing you?

2

the sexual story
God intended for you

What comes into our minds when we think about God is the most important thing about us.

A. W. Tozer, The Knowledge of the Holy

God and sex are connected. As author Dr. Juli Slattery says, "Every sexual question begins and ends with questions about God."[1]

Jasmine struggled with that connection. She had been taught both at home and at church that sex was for marriage only. But that didn't seem to affect her behavior very much. She started having sex at fifteen, had her first child at nineteen, by twenty-six had slept with more men and women than she could remember, and was filing papers for her second divorce. Something wasn't working. She couldn't forget what she'd been taught about what God says about sex, but she couldn't connect that with where her heart was struggling today. She told me, "I think I need to rewire my brain when it comes to sex. The part of me that wants sex and the part of my brain that thinks about God aren't connected. I'm confused."

Victor was mad at God. When marrying Lizza, he'd committed to being sexually faithful to her, and he had kept that vow. No cheating, no porn. But for several years now, sex had been rare, difficult, and emotionless. He couldn't imagine living like this for the rest of his life. How long could he hold out? It seemed God was going back on His promise of a good sex life if he remained faithful to his wife. He was considering giving up and looking for sex elsewhere.

Both Mariana and Stephan had been married before and had been deeply wounded in the ways their marriages had ended. Mariana had always been a strong Christian, while Stephan had recently returned to church after some years of living anything but a Christian lifestyle. They were talking about marriage, but their complicated relationship histories predicted big challenges if they moved forward. Was their baggage too much for a marriage to work? Was the connection they wanted now even possible long-term?

Perhaps you're unsettled too. Maybe the God part and the sex part of your brain seem disconnected, like they do for Jasmine. Or like Victor, "obeying" God in the area of sexuality feels antithetical to what you need and desire. Or like Mariana and Stephan, your heart wonders if the past is too big for God to really do anything with. Part of you suspects that something's missing, but what is it?

Christian psychiatrist Dr. Curt Thompson hints at what's missing:

> Our Christian faith seems to be mostly a cognitive assent to a series of rational beliefs that don't seem to help us resolve our family conflicts, our struggles with sexuality, our sense of isolation, or our ongoing burden of shame and guilt.[2]

As important as rational beliefs about God are, they're not enough. To be able to write a new chapter of your sexual story, you will also need to bring the emotional feeling part of you to the party and to your relationship with God.

To listen to much of the classical Christian teaching, you might conclude that God hates sex. He might put up with it as a necessary act when husband and wife are wanting to have a child, but you imagine the Holy Spirit leaving the room when you make love. And to top it off, Paul said you better buck up and give it to your spouse or you're displeasing God (common interpretation of 1 Corinthians 7:2–5. I don't believe that's what Paul was saying, by the way. More on that in chapter 8). But as one husband said to me, "Pity sex is the worst." And I might add that duty sex is just as bad.

> You will also need to bring the emotional feeling part of you to the party and to your relationship with God.

You might also imagine God saying, "You better not like sex too much; it might get you into trouble." You've got to wrestle your sexual drives to the ground. A really good Christian doesn't want much sex or think about it very much. God might seem cruel and arbitrary to create you as a sexual being and then expect you to "save yourself for marriage."

You've probably heard that sex was God's idea. That's true, but it's a left-brain logical truth. The left-brain/right-brain understanding of how our internal system works helps put many things into perspective. Your left brain functions in a largely logical, linear, and verbal way. Your right brain deals more with emotions and feelings, and is nonverbal, nonlinear, and primarily sensory.

Your left brain may know a lot of "truth" about God and sex, but your right brain doesn't automatically line up with that and it asks very different questions. Questions like, Why did God create you as a sexual being? Is He taunting you, giving you a sex drive and withholding from you a way to have it satisfied? Is He cruel, demanding you live in a way that seems impossible or perhaps even harmful? And what if you've already messed up a lot? It seems a risky endeavor indeed for God to have created humans as sexual beings. What was He up to? And why would He care about your sexuality now?

Considering such questions gets us closer to an understanding of why sex is never just sex. There's a lot more going on than just biology. Here we look at the origin story to trump all origin stories—yours.

Who Are You?

Before you were a glint in your mommy's or daddy's eyes, you were a glint in God's eyes. You may have heard that human beings are created in God's image. "So God created man in his own image, in the image of God he created him; male and female he created them" (Genesis 1:27).

You, yes you, are carrying the image of the living God, the image of the one who holds the universe in His hands, who created everything, who is love. You are not God; the universe does not revolve around you. But you are made by Him and are like Him in very important ways.

What does that mean?

Consider what we know about God. Early Christians came to understand God as existing in three Persons: God the Father, God the Son (the eternal Word, Jesus), and God the Holy Spirit. The trinity is one of those mysteries we can't completely get our logical left brains around.

We are also told to think of God as one God. And He is. "Hear, O Israel: The LORD our God, the LORD is one" (Deuteronomy 6:4). Jesus quoted this Old Testament Scripture (see Mark 12:29). This foundational proclamation is still prayed daily by Orthodox Jews. Father, Son, and Spirit are so close in relationship to one another, so intimate, so united, that though they are separate personalities, they are one.

God is relational within Himself. Intimacy, oneness with the other members of the Godhead, is part of His very nature. He can't *not* be relational. He can't *not* be intimate.

That's really what love is. You may know the Scripture "God is love" (1 John 4:8). Love doesn't, can't, exist in isolation. Love needs a beloved. Within Himself God expresses infinite love between Father, Son, and Spirit. Just as every other aspect of God is infinite, His relational nature and the love within Himself is infinite. We can say He experiences and exemplifies infinite intimacy within Himself. And love cannot remain self-contained; it must extend itself outward. God wanted a family to love and to receive love from. So He created human beings—He created you.

> God created you with the need, desire, and capacity for intimacy.

You, created in God's image, are a relational being too. You can't *not* be relational. It's part of your nature. Love it or hate it, you were made to be deeply, intimately connected. To be fully seen and known.

In creating you in His image, God created you with the need, desire, and capacity for intimacy.

Need for intimacy? (Fireworks. Red flags. Fight/flight/freeze responses in your body and your brain—*Why? Ouch! No! Yes! Yes, please!! Never!* Soul hunger. Deep angst. Ambivalence . . .)

For just a moment put away those automatic reactions. Try to consciously set aside all the devastation and destruction your experience of intimacy or lack thereof has brought, all the ways you have been harmed by or have harmed others, all the feelings of emptiness that thinking about intimacy may engender. Point your mind back to what we know about God and His creation of human beings in His image.

Without a doubt, God knew what would happen when He created human beings the way He did, with the need for intimacy. He could look ahead and see how humans would confuse intimacy and sex (more on that shortly), and all the horrendous things evil would do with this need. God could see and feel the impact of everything that sex and intimacy would mean for humans—sex trafficking, sexual violence, porn addiction, sexless marriages, STDs, and all the other horrendous outcomes, not to mention the isolation and loneliness. Yet He chose to create His human children in His image anyway, as relational and sexual beings.

The only conclusion can be that God considered intimacy so critical to His own nature, so core to who He is, that He could not create humans in His image without building into them the need, desire, and capacity for intimacy. That's what "in His image" means, in part. And He considered the risk worth it.

In our angst, you or I might disagree. For all the struggle sex and intimacy have brought, you might agree with Victor when he told me that it would be better if that part of him were eliminated or was never there in the first place. Part of you might wish that sex were just sex, that God had created us with biological drives like the animals, where sex was for procreation only and didn't have the emotional, relational, and spiritual weight that it does. Like Jasmine, you might wish God's feelings about sex didn't seem so different from your feelings about sex. Or like Mariana and

Stephan, you might question whether the desire for intimacy is worth all the work it will take in the face of all the junk.

But sex and intimacy do have that weight because that's how God created us—in His image. And because that's how God created you, sex feels very close—*is* very close—to the core of who you are. Your sexuality does not define you. You are a child of God, and living out of your identity as His child is always best and most fulfilling. But we can't talk about sex without addressing who you are in the deepest part of you.

Let's look closer at that hunger for intimacy that marks us as like God.

Intimacy and You

What have you done with your need, desire, and capacity for intimacy? We'll get to the specific ways sex is connected to intimacy in a bit, but right now, let's consider the part of you that longs to be connected to someone, to see and be fully seen, to know and be fully known.

You might have closed yourself off years or even decades ago, consciously or unconsciously concluding that being known was too dangerous. Your need and desire for intimacy made you too vulnerable, so you've fallen into a lifestyle of hiding. Human beings have been hiding ever since the garden of Eden (see Genesis 3), and practice makes perfect—for humans in general and for you. It's lonely behind your walls, but you can't imagine doing anything else. And after all these years, you don't even know how to do anything *but* hide.

You might have a history of running from one relationship or situation to another. Those relationships may or may not have been sexual, but they keep happening. Your internal world feels ravenously empty and you keep seeking for someone or something to fill you up. You quickly become "hooked" when someone seems to have what you're looking for, but you discard them relatively quickly when they let you down. And they always do.

Or perhaps you're trying desperately to live "right." If you're married, that means no sexual behavior except with your spouse. But you feel doomed. Sex with your spouse isn't cutting it. Or as a single, your only godly choice seems to be squelching your hunger for intimacy, and that gets exhausting. Is this the best you can hope for?

Maybe you've concluded, perhaps unconsciously, that intimacy might work for others, but it isn't for you. You've tried, but you keep running into a brick wall. You might blame others. Or perhaps you're like a man named David who wrote me, "I'm too broken to hope for any intimacy in my future. I just have to find a way to survive." You feel incapable of real intimacy, so you fall into some addiction that takes the edge off temporarily.

The ways you've dealt with your need for intimacy connect deeply with your sexual story. Here are a few questions to help you reflect on your experience around intimacy:

- Have you ever felt understood by those closest to you? Look back at your life for moments when someone—a parent, friend, spouse, etc.—really "got" you.
- Have you even been aware of your deep hunger for intimacy? What emotions come up as you consider this part of your story?
- When you have risked being vulnerable, letting someone see you, how have they responded? Did that experience make you more or less willing to try being vulnerable again?

- Which of your "bad behaviors" might be related to your need for intimacy? Have you tried to drown that desire with substances such as alcohol? Assuage it with illegitimate sex, or porn, or an affair?
- How effective have your attempts at fulfilling your need for intimacy been? How have you felt after such attempts?
- Who do you blame for how your attempts at intimacy have worked out? Yourself? Others? Perhaps even God?

Considering these parts of your heart and your experience may leave you feeling disrupted, worse rather than better. The empty well is so deep it hurts to go there or even consider doing so. Rest assured, that feeling is temporary, and normal. It's what looking at your sexual story is all about: revealing the pain in order to heal it. This will be key to writing the next chapter of your story.

What's Love Got to Do with Intimacy and Sex?

Intimacy and sex are related but they're not the same. Too often people say one when they mean the other. And you may have already realized that going for sex when you need intimacy doesn't guarantee that need will be filled.

My friend is a chaplain at a large women's prison. She told me that many of the women there think "sex" when you say "love." Perhaps sex and love are somewhat confused in your mind also. Perhaps a parent or other older person lured you with the promise of love in grooming you before sexually abusing you. Or you thought "love" when you were noticed and at least superficially cared about when you offered your body sexually. You might have experienced sex as a way to get validation; it meant you were a "real" man or woman. Perhaps you've never experienced someone being truly for you, fighting for you because you are valuable as a person, not because of what they want from you. Sex has become a way to feel temporarily connected or powerful, to get a momentary surge of brain chemicals that lets you feel special. But it never lasts.

God's perspective on love is bigger and better than that. As God intended it, sex and intimacy overlap within a permanent loving covenant relationship. That three-fold cord—sex, intimacy, and covenant marriage—is the earthly object lesson of the infinite loving intimacy He experiences within Himself and that He desires to have with us. That's a really big thought, and it's so different from what many of us have experienced.

As God intended it, sex and intimacy overlap within a permanent loving covenant relationship.

The idea of love has lost much of its glory in contemporary culture. Love is confused with sex, tolerance, or nice feelings. But since God's love is the original, the source, consider that His relationship with us is based on covenant, not contract. It's not, "I'll love you if you make me feel good." Or, "I'll love you if you do what I say." Or, "I'll love you if I feel like it today." God bases His relationship with us on who He is, not on what we do. His love for you is both tough and tender. He is for you. There's nothing you can do that could make Him love you any more or any less. That's covenant. That kind of love creates the safety needed for you to experience the transformation He desires for you. How you respond does have consequences, but your response never changes His love for you.

The generosity of God loving us this way, we who are so "other" than Him, boggles the mind. The coming together of a man and woman in covenant marriage, so different from each other but building oneness in body, mind, and soul, is the context in which sex becomes the physical object lesson of God's love for us.

Imagine for a moment the very best sexual experience you can possibly dream of. You may or may not have experienced anything remotely like it. You may have to put aside your frustration or angst or PTSD momentarily. But based on what you know or imagine or desire when it comes to good sex, what words come to mind? They might be words such as exciting, safe, fulfilling, connected, warm, adventurous, committed, generous, intimate, romantic, comforting, mutual, affirming, exhilarating, satisfying, life-giving.

That's how God feels about sex. Sex was His idea and His creation, and it was—and is—very good. The very reason you can imagine those good things about sex is because of the way God created you—and sex—in the first place. (And if you can't imagine sex being good, don't quit now. We'll get there.)

Authors Allender and Longman say it this way: "God loves sex. He conceived, created, and blessed the process by which our bodies know and are known through desire, arousal, foreplay, intercourse, orgasm, and rest. Sex is meant by God to be one of the bridge experiences between earth and heaven."[3] The very first directive God gave humans in the garden of Eden had to do with sex. Be fruitful, multiply, and fill the earth with more humans (see Genesis 1:28). As Dr. David Lamb says, "God's first command is basically, 'Have a lot of sex.'"[4]

That's a wonderful picture. Sex in the context of the three-fold cord with intimacy and covenant marriage is glorious. (To be clear, marriage is not the goal of the Christian life; Christlikeness is. You can be sexually whole whether you're married or single. More about this in chapter 9.)

The Song of Songs is a beautiful Hebrew love poem, very erotic, very explicit. It portrays sexual desire, sexual pursuit, arousal, foreplay, intercourse, orgasm, and satisfaction. If you know a little of the imagery, you can find allusions (or direct reference) to erect penis, aroused vagina, testicles, oral sex, vaginal intercourse, semen, vaginal fluids—it's all there, in the Bible. And it's all unadulterated goodness. The lovers are totally enraptured with each other, safe, unashamed, exclusive, committed, emptied, filled, and satisfied.

Have you ever had sex like that?

Perhaps the fact that many people haven't is one reason the church has often spiritualized this book of the Bible too much. For humans, sex has lost its glory. Yes, Song of Songs also applies to the totally committed relationship Christ has with His people. But right now we're talking about how God feels about sex. And based on this biblical depiction we would say He's totally for it. It's not that we want too much out of sex, it's that we settle for too little.

Some people I talk with can't read the Song of Songs. "Reading that makes my skin crawl," says Christine. If that's triggering for you, don't start reading the Bible there. That can be saved for later.

Before I got married I knew my many hang-ups around sex would impair the sexual relationship between my husband and me unless I dealt with them. So along with all the work of preparing for a wedding, I marinated in the Song of Songs. I lost count of how many times I read that book, slowly, during those few months. And my wedding night was good, very good.

But what about your experience? Remember, we're looking at your sexual story with honesty and compassion. How well have the sexual experiences you've had reflected that glory—that best-possible sexual experience you imagined or tried to imagine, that enrapturing one-flesh-ness that God intended for you?

- Did you learn about sex as only biology? Did those who taught you about sex connect it to intimacy and loving covenant relationship?
- Have you experienced sex and intimacy together? If you've experienced sex without intimacy, how did you feel afterward?
- If you've experienced sex that's been less than satisfying, what was lacking? What are you desiring more of?
- Even if your analytical left brain believes this picture of glorious sex is true, how does your intuitive right brain feel about it?

Intimacy, Sex, and You

God built you with the need, desire, and capacity for intimacy. You cannot thrive and become healed and whole without being connected, seen, and known. This applies regardless of your relationship status. He created the holes in our souls to make us hungry for true intimacy—with others, and with Him. He designed that hunger to keep us seeking until we find our deepest satisfaction ultimately in Him. As Saint Augustine said, "You have made us for yourself, O Lord, and our hearts are restless until they rest in You."

You can live without sex, but you can't live, or at least live well, without intimacy.

No, I can't live without sex! That's why I'm in this fix. You're not alone in feeling that way. Saint Augustine felt that way too, and also said, "Oh Lord, give me chastity, but do not give it yet."

We know Jesus lived as a human being while on earth with all the sex hormones we have. He never married, never had sex. Yet He was the most fully alive human being to ever live. Would He have been more fully alive if He had gotten married or had sex? Certainly not.

But Jesus needed and sought intimacy. And like us, His human experience of intimacy was mixed. He experienced times of true connection with His inner circle of disciples and with friends such as Mary, Martha, and Lazarus. And He also experienced deep loneliness, betrayal, misunderstanding, and harm from those He sought intimacy with. He understands your ambivalence, fear, desire, need, and frustration.

Cultivating true intimacy with God is absolutely vital to you becoming sexually whole.

Jesus also lived in daily intimacy with His Father. He couldn't have made it any other way. And that's the only way you'll make it too. The only chance you have of growing in sexual wholeness is truly connecting with God, not only with your left brain, but also with your right brain, your whole self. Cultivating true intimacy with God is absolutely vital to you becoming sexually whole and to writing the next chapter of your sexual story.

This may stir up mixed feelings. It sounds good. Sort of. Part of you may want that kind of connection with God, but another part of you deeply distrusts that it's even possible, or that it would be good. It sounds too spiritual to make any real difference in your sex life. The best you might hope for is God's mercy. You're not completely sure you want Him that close. He might mess with you. You're too embarrassed or ashamed to let Him that close. And what if He takes away your sex drive? Or leaves you with your sex drive but you never experience a "good" outlet for it? Or He "forces" you into pursuing intimacy with a spouse who wounds you? (God never forces you. Please keep reading.)

What do you do with those right-brain feelings that seem out of sync with the left-brain things you logically "know"? You may have tried stuffing or ignoring them for a long time, and found that doesn't work. Neurobiologically, your right brain is more in charge and will override your logical left brain almost every time.

Becoming more whole requires that those different parts of you become more integrated. How does that happen? Instead of ignoring your subjective feelings about sex, intimacy, relationship, and God, let me invite you to be curious about them and bring them to Jesus. The guided reflections at the end of each chapter provide a pathway for you to do just that: to start bringing your right brain into His presence. There's no "right" way you should be feeling. Honesty and compassion, remember?

Your individual sexual story happens within a larger story that started with glory. That larger story is the way you were designed for perfect intimacy. But like all good love stories, this story has a villain. And it's there to which we turn our focus in the next chapter.

IN MY HOUSE

You're at home in a familiar room, perhaps your office or your bedroom. It only takes a moment to realize something is different. You thought you were alone, but Someone is already there, making Himself at home. You're surprised.

As much as your heart leaped when He said "I'm coming to your house," you're not sure you can do this. You're a bit ambivalent about His presence. The longing you feel is mixed with skepticism, sadness, anxiety, self-contempt. Someone seeing you the way His eyes do feels uncomfortable.

Your story is messy. Maybe He doesn't really see you as much as you thought. You'll try to respect your Guest and make Him welcome.

You can tell that He senses your angst, including your ambivalence about His very presence in your familiar room. Without His saying so, you get the message that He anticipated your mixed feelings.

His feelings don't seem at all mixed. He doesn't seem bothered by your reluctance to go to the place where you need Him the most. His silence isn't the least bit awkward, but warm and inviting. Your soul feels penetrated. He's just present, impossible to ignore but full of kindness.

Your ambivalence about His presence hasn't made Him leave, and you also sense He won't stay any longer than you truly want Him to. The next move will have to be yours.

You're not sure what to do. Maybe if you tell Him how messed up and upset you are, even upset with Him, He'll go away. A sentence escapes your lips, and then another, and another. "How could You . . . ? Why didn't You . . . ? I can't . . . ! I don't understand. You don't understand . . . !" He doesn't interrupt. His eyes remain as kind as ever. He doesn't leave.

The dam of emotions in you lets go. Your anger, pain, fear, frustration—none of it seems to alter the invitation in His gaze.

His presence seems to open up the deepest places in your soul and pull things out of those places, things you had forgotten about or never even knew were there.

You sense no impatience from Him. He's here for as long as it takes. Even if it's a very long time.

Once you've said all you want to say, more than you thought there was to say, your Visitor's eyes still show the same warmth. You've never known Him in this way before. Come to think of it, have you ever really known Him? And you've never felt known by Him like this. Yes, He does see you.

He'd like to come back again. You begin to wonder if maybe this could be the start of something you'd hoped for but had stopped believing could truly happen.

Your sense of His presence begins to fade. It's not that He left; it's that you have experienced as much as you can take for today. You feel a quietness inside even as you're more aware of your longing for Him than ever.

You breathe deeply. A part of you dares to believe it might end up being okay.

Questions to Discuss or Contemplate

- How do you feel about the fact that God created you with the need, desire, and capacity for intimacy?
- How has that need for intimacy played out in your story, specifically in your sexual story?
- Have you confused sex, intimacy, and love in your mind? How are they connected? How are they different?
- When you imagine God's part in your story, what feelings come up? Not what you think about Him or believe you should feel, but what does your right brain actually sense about Him?

intimacy gone wrong:
how sex has lost its glory

*To be human is to be infected with this phenomenon we call
shame.*

Dr. Curt Thompson, The Soul of Shame

Reina couldn't stop crying. As a child, she had watched her stepfather brutalize her mother. When she finally got old enough, she
threatened to go to the police, and that made the physical violence
stop, mostly. But the violence in her soul didn't stop. She concluded that men were bad, incapable of true love and intimacy,
so she started sexually connecting with girls. When she married
Thomas, she hoped that would change; it didn't. Thomas had his
own issues and rarely connected with her emotionally or sexually.

Reina had tried to cope by white-knuckling it to behave "right."
And it wasn't working. Her demands on Thomas only made him
withdraw further. Her two close friends had let her down and
she wasn't willing to risk friendship again. God? She kept crying out to Him and it seemed He wouldn't answer. "I can't do
this anymore. I want those parts of me to go away." She despised
her inner desires for affectionate play and real connection. If she

could just kill off little-girl Reina and grow up, maybe she could make life work.

God's glorious design for intimacy had gone horribly wrong for Reina. Has it gone wrong for you?

Let's pan out and look again at the grand epic of which your story is a part. God is love, and He experiences infinite intimacy within Himself between Father, Son, and Spirit. He created human beings in His image, with the need, desire, and capacity for intimacy. Biblically, Genesis 1 and 2 describe how God originally created things to be: human beings in a perfect environment experiencing perfect intimacy with each other and with Him, "naked and . . . not ashamed" (Genesis 2:25). No coverings over their bodies, but also no coverings over their minds or hearts. Completely seen and known.

And the last two chapters of the Bible, Revelation 21 and 22, describe how God will re-create things to be in the end. It's a picture of Eden restored, endless intimacy and goodness. Human beings in a perfect environment. The whole scene is described as a wedding (see Revelation 21:2, 9). "God himself will be with them as their God" (Revelation 21:3). "They will see his face" (Revelation 22:4). Human beings, you and me, completely seen and known.

But what happens between the first two and the last two chapters of the Bible? That's the drama, the ultimate love story with the ultimate Hero, the ultimate villain, and the best of all beloveds—you.

Intimacy Gone Wrong

Stage left: Enter the serpent. In the very next verse after "naked and not ashamed" the villain shows himself, intent on stealing, killing, and destroying. Humankind falls. And the very first thing humans do is hide.

> Then the eyes of both were opened, and they knew that they were naked. And they sewed fig leaves together and made themselves loincloths. And they heard the sound of the LORD God walking in the garden in the cool of the day, and the man and his wife hid themselves from the presence of the LORD God among the trees of the garden.
>
> Genesis 3:7–8

Can you imagine anything more tragic? Perfect, glorious intimacy, and it's all gone. Instead of "naked and not ashamed" the man and woman find themselves hiding in the bushes trying to cover themselves with leaves. The voice of their Creator, whom they had previously enjoyed and welcomed, now causes them to shrink in fear. The whole fall of humankind could be summed up in the phrase "intimacy gone wrong."

For the fallen man and woman shame becomes their constant companion. Shame becomes our constant companion as well. Christian psychiatrist Dr. Curt Thompson describes how:

> Shame's presence is ubiquitous and inserts itself into the genetic material of the human storytelling endeavor. One way to envision shame is as a personal attendant. Your shame attendant's intention is not good, is not to care for you but rather to infuse nonverbal and verbal elements of judgment into every moment of your life.[1]

But remember, humans are created with the need for intimacy. That need has not gone away. It's part of our very nature. And now shame complicates things exponentially. How am I going to get my need for intimacy met with my shame attendant derisively commenting on every moment of my life? And of course the serpent, the villain who started this whole debacle, is ready with any number of diabolical "solutions." And true to his crafty, deceptive, and thoroughly evil nature, his solutions only serve to steal, kill, and destroy. We are starving for intimacy and often eagerly consume the junk food the serpent offers, only to soon discover it's just a slower and even more painful death.

How far we have fallen. As humans try to pursue intimacy, the serpent entices them, us, to turn from glory to the dark side. And sometimes that darkness is very dark indeed.

Ted Bundy was a serial killer who kidnapped, raped, and murdered at least thirty young women, likely many more. In 1989 at age forty-two he was executed after receiving three death sentences for three of the murders. The afternoon prior to his execution he granted Dr. James Dobson an interview. Bundy's motivations for that interview have understandably been questioned. But the darkness he describes resulting from pornography is chilling.

> Once you become addicted to it, and I look at this as a kind of addiction, you look for more potent, more explicit, more graphic kinds of material. Like an addiction, you keep craving something which is harder and gives you a greater sense of excitement, until you reach the point where the pornography only goes so far—that jumping off point where you begin to think maybe actually doing it will give you that which is just beyond reading about it and looking at it. . . . I've lived in prison for a long time now, and I've met a lot of men who were motivated to commit violence. Without exception, every one of them was deeply involved in pornography—deeply consumed by the addiction.[2]

The point is not to see Bundy as an authority; he is not. It is also important to note that there are countless women and men addicted to porn who do not become serial killers. The point is to gaze for a horrifying moment at how bad evil really is, at what evil tries to do, and the lengths to which it will go with intimacy gone wrong. Evil has masterfully exploited human sexuality in its campaign of terror and destruction.

I spoke this week with a young man wrestling to integrate his relationship with his girlfriend, whom he loves greatly, and the darkness he feels from trauma in his past. "I can only see a small flicker of light in my soul, surrounded by something so vile and grossly dark inside. I'm trying to walk out of this dark place but I'm not sure I can."

This young man is no Ted Bundy. He's a churchgoer who is staring at the effects in his own heart of intimacy gone wrong.

In thirty seconds you could probably name a dozen categories of intimacy gone wrong, arenas where evil has exploited the sexual nature of humankind in some way to cause harm, suffering, and destruction. Those would include the "gross" categories of child sexual abuse, rape (including its use as a weapon of cultural manipulation), domestic violence (including marital rape), human sex trafficking, and child pornography. But additional categories include sexless marriages, sexually transmitted infections, abortion, affairs, multiple sexual partners (whether promiscuity or periods of monogamy with each), divorce, single parenthood, shacking up, all pornography, bondage (all BDSM practices), sex for hire, gender dysphoria, same-sex behaviors, and sexualization of children.

These categories are not all equal in destructiveness, nor is the list exhaustive. Some of these categories seem more connected to humans' need for intimacy than others. Some are more the result of intimacy needs gone wrong and some speak more of a particular behavior or experience.

You might question the inclusion of some of these categories as intimacy gone wrong. Abortion, for example. But does any woman wake up one day and say, "Today I'm going to kill my baby"? As important as the discussion is about what happens once the pregnancy test is positive, there's much less discussion about what happens six or ten weeks earlier. Who's helping that (often) young woman address the matters in her own heart, or perhaps helping her see the means of exploitation that led her into a situation where she becomes pregnant in the first place?

Divorce is another example. There are many reasons for it. But when that couple first said "I do," they were expecting lasting connection, goodness, and intimacy. Now what? What baggage around relationships and intimacy did they bring into the marriage? What unfilled needs for intimacy drove them apart? Someone's (or both partners') bad behavior, often in the arena of intimacy gone wrong, rips apart and destroys the union they had entered into hoping for happily ever after.

Remember the three-fold cord we described in the last chapter? As God intended it, sex, intimacy, and covenant exist together in a strong and life-giving marriage. But evil has so disrupted that three-fold cord that it's hardly recognizable. There are plenty of marriages where no intimacy exists whether sex is happening or not. And there's plenty of intimacy gone wrong for those in any relationship status. It's just more stealing, killing, and destroying.

The categories in the list above are all in some way an outgrowth of intimacy gone wrong, looking for love in all the wrong places. Sex becomes about self-gratification, power and control, oppression or perversion or pain. Brianna, who we met earlier, recalls with horror the look in Marty's eyes when he first realized he had caused her physical pain during sex. For a moment, before catching himself, he briefly exulted in her pain; his expression was a self-congratulatory "I did that!" In that moment he was expressing pure evil; in his case an expression of how porn had damaged his brain.

But evil has one sinister coup de grace, one final deadly blow in which he seeks to blame the Originator of intimacy for all the mayhem he himself has caused. Evil has been busy planting evidence through enticing sometimes well-meaning religious organizations or leaders to cloud our need for intimacy with an even thicker layer of shame. Fighting over the sin list can make God seem like a tyrant. And when Christian leaders fall into sexual sin, the family of God often seems the least authentic or helpful place anyone needing help would want to go. Men and women, young or old, married or single, feel left to sort out their sexuality on their own without the only One who could bring true transformation, healing, and intimacy.

Sometimes powerful leaders or spouses (usually husbands) sexually exploit and harm (usually) women or other vulnerable individuals using God-talk. If that's part of your story, such abuse in the name of God seriously distorts your internal picture of God and the ability of your left brain to believe Him or your right brain to trust Him, or to even want to. As Dr. Diane Langberg, psychologist and international speaker who works with trauma survivors, caregivers, and clergy, says, "The God that they think of as being real is actually false. When you're told about God using His words and [then you're] abused, there's no teaching in there of the true God. It isn't there."[3]

> **This is how far evil will go to separate human beings from the One who originally created them with the need for intimacy and the only One who can restore them to it.**

Imagine the very worst possible sexual experience, whether or not it's one you've actually had yourself. What words come to mind? They might be something like painful, exploitative, destructive, one-sided, empty, no intimacy, coerced, using or being used, depersonalizing, violent, triggering, abusive, deceitful, damaging, shame-filled, or unsatisfying. That's a description of evil. That's intimacy gone wrong.

This is how bad evil is. This is what evil does with the image of God in human beings, specifically our need for intimacy. And this is how far evil will go to separate human beings from the One who originally created them with the need for intimacy and the only One who can restore them to it.

How far we have fallen indeed.

Intimacy Gone Wrong for You

Now we turn our attention from the gross darkness "out there" and flip the camera around for a selfie. I encourage you again to consider your own story with both honesty and compassion, the way Jesus sees you. You might have read the previous paragraphs and thought, *I'm not that bad. If that's what evil does with sex, I might just need a little tune-up, but I'll be okay.* Certainly behaviors have consequences, and some behaviors have more obvious and destructive consequences than others. For example, no sleeping around means no sexually transmitted infections. Okay, you've got this under control. But do you really? Have you fully addressed the unseen areas in your own soul?

Or you might have read those previous paragraphs and felt triggered. Your brain can't forget the things that have happened to you or the things you've done to yourself or others. Perhaps you've lived some of those worst possible sexual experiences and you feel damaged beyond repair. Yup, it's that bad, so it might feel "safer" to patch up your masks and search for even better ways to hide. But how's that working for you?

You probably picked up this book because in some way intimacy has gone wrong in your story. Where has it gone wrong for you? Where is your story different from the glory story around sex and intimacy we talked about in the last chapter? And who is the real villain in your story?

A great place to start is to consider who you blame for the unwholeness you sense in your soul around sex and intimacy. Who's the bad guy? Your father for sexually molesting you? Some older classmate who showed you porn? Friends or "friends with benefits" for expecting or demanding sex, or for being so hard to hook up with? Your spouse for demanding sex or for withholding sex? The cultural norms you picked up that led you to follow a sexual ethic of "anything goes"? Purity culture in the church, for making you either rebel against it or hate sex? God, for making you a sexual being?

> **Where has intimacy gone wrong for you?**

But when your contempt turns on yourself, it's even worse. You may secretly despise that six-year-old you for giving in so easily to sexual abuse, or that ten-year-old you for following your friend to look at porn and getting hooked. You hate your teenage self for being either so out of control or so naïve, or your present unending neediness that keeps you running from relationship to relationship. You look with contempt on the part of you that wants more from your marriage than your spouse seems willing or able to give. Or you hate the way you hide, making intimacy seemingly impossible even if you have someone willing to see and know you.

You may cover over that self-contempt with bravado, anger, acting out, or good works. You may wear yourself out pretending everything is okay. But part of you wishes you were different, that certain parts of your story hadn't happened. Or like Reina, you wish parts of you would just go away.

You're not alone. You come by that self-contempt honestly. Dr. Dan Allender writes, "Evil hates what God reveals in and through the creation of humanity, especially with regard to gender and sexuality. Nothing brings evil greater delight or power than to foul our joy in being a man or a woman through sexual harm or gender confusion on the one hand or dogmatism on the other."[4] And the shame perpetrated in a moment seems sticky enough to last a lifetime.

> **Shame perpetrated in a moment seems sticky enough to last a lifetime.**

You've been harmed, and you've also harmed others. No, you didn't wake up one day and decide, *Today I think I'll damage someone's sense of self, exploit their trust, and cause them a lifetime's worth of shame.* But in your attempts to meet your own need for intimacy you used others. The templates in your own brain resulted in you objectifying, fearing, or hiding from others. You acted out distorted fantasies or desires. You've heard it said that hurting people hurt people. Perhaps you showed a younger child porn, enticed someone into an illegitimate sexual liaison, coerced or forced someone into having sex, hid from your spouse sexually because of your own junk (saying no to sex does not itself equal sexual harm), or in some other way perpetrated sexual harm on another vulnerable human.[5] The possibilities are endless.

After being in that hotel room with a married man, I had to face the lies I had come to believe, the wounds I had accumulated, and the empty places still unfilled in my soul. What lies, wounds, and empty places are you living with? There are ways you've been harmed. There are ways you've harmed yourself. And there are ways you've harmed others. You've been sinned against, and you've also sinned against yourself, God, and others. Where has intimacy gone wrong for you?

- When you feel shame around your sexuality or gender, how old do you feel? What was happening around that age that may have harmed you sexually?
- How were you "discipled" sexually? What lies or distortions became embedded in your soul around sex or sexuality as a result?
- What experiences led you to feel exploited, used, or objectified? In what ways has anger or entitlement become attached to your sexuality?
- How has your shame attendant been impacting your sexuality? What hurtful messages have continued to sound in your brain?
- What decisions have you made sexually, or what actions have you taken, that have harmed you? In what ways have you been your own worst enemy?
- What have you done in grasping for intimacy that has brought harm to others? Who has been negatively impacted by how you have stewarded your sexuality? How do you feel about that?
- How have the lies, wounds, and empty places in your soul around intimacy and sexuality negatively impacted your view of God and your willingness to connect with Him?

What's the Villain After?

So what's the big deal with evil anyway? What is Satan really after?

Theologically, if the conflict between the kingdom of God and the kingdom of darkness were about power or territory, this cosmic war would have been over a long time ago. But the real battlefield is over the human soul. And we know the end of the story: (spoiler alert) Jesus wins! So why wouldn't God wrap things up right now? Or better yet, why did He allow all this misery and destruction in the first place? If He cares and He's all powerful, how could He let it get this bad?

Human words fail to adequately answer such questions, but the best way to think about this goes back to the love story archetype. Such stories work because they speak to the way we are made. Any good love story has a hero, a heroine, and a villain. And in those stories, what is the villain after? In a true love story the villain is after the heroine's heart. And the hero is also after the beloved's heart. It's her love, worship, and devotion that he will risk everything for. He counts everything else as rubbish, he's willing to lose it all, if he gains the heart of his beloved.

What part of that love story archetype resonates with you? Does your heart long to be seen and "worshiped" by your beloved, to feel like you have all of her? Do you long to be fought for, romanced, desired, and cherished that much, knowing with absolute certainty that you are number one to your hero?

Perhaps your heart is so jaded by intimacy gone wrong that this all feels embarrassingly sentimental and completely "not me." You hate love stories anyway. If so, it's okay, even healthy, to dismiss the often cheesy human depictions of love. And truly, the kind of love we're talking about is anything but cheesy. It's fierce, resilient, even violent when necessary.

In this story to end all stories, regardless of your gender or relationship status, the amazing thing is that you are the beloved. It's your heart that both the Hero and the villain are after. The villain has studied you. He knows you better than you know yourself. He knows your Achilles' heel, exactly what wounds to exploit in drawing in your allegiance. He knows how to hook you and then degrade you, hoping to draw you so deeply into his camp that you're lost to the Hero forever.

But your Hero has already won the war. The unanswered question is, will He win your heart? Remember, the villain's coup de grace strategy is to get you to see your Hero as the villain. And you're not going to give your heart to one who your right brain believes is out to get you. This is not a primarily left-brain exercise, as important as facts about God are. God could command or "force" obedience, but a commanded love is not love.

> Your Hero wants so much more for you. In your future as His beloved, He sees a truly glorious "happily ever after."

By its very nature this kind of love can only be freely given, otherwise it's not love. What does it take to win your heart? Sometimes it seems our hearts can be won by any shiny trinket that can fizzle out quicker than a child's sparkler on the 4th of July. All it takes is a box of chocolates, a roller-coaster rush, a moment of internal relief from shame. It's like the stereotypical kidnapper offering a child candy before pulling them into the van.

But your Hero wants so much more for you. In your future as His beloved, He sees a truly glorious "happily ever after." He doesn't want you to give Him your heart for a trinket. You're too valuable for that. He's after your eternal unreserved affection, worship, and love. And He's also after the heart of every other blind and exploited human being on earth.

Such ideas may not fully satisfy our legitimate questions about evil, but they can help.

The State of Your Heart

What has this exploration of intimacy gone wrong stirred up in you?

You might feel as though this darkness is far removed from you. All you're after is a little personal satisfaction, a little comfort, a momentary relief. That's not too much to ask, is it? You're not after anything evil. Marriage wasn't anywhere in sight, culture gave you no other options, and you felt you needed sex. That person said yes; it was totally consensual. Maybe not ideal, but it was the best you could do.

Or you feel you've never watched porn that's overly degrading or evil. Maybe you identify with Pastor James, whose spouse usually shows little interest in sex. He occasionally watches videos of sex between a seemingly warm husband and a wife who wants him. He imagines it makes him less demanding. He knows getting sexual gratification from someone other than his wife (even virtually) is wrong, but he rationalizes that it's not hurting his marriage very much and that he can keep himself from harming anyone else. (By the way, more sex with his wife would not cure Pastor James's porn use. And it *is* hurting his marriage.)

It might be for you that intimacy gone wrong seems too big a mountain to climb. You feel like Gloria, who had sex with her first real crush at age sixteen, and a series of boyfriends and threesomes followed. Shame and abuse in various combinations followed her everywhere, even into one marriage after another. Her body, mind, and heart seem damaged beyond repair. Her left brain believes God heals and forgives, but her right brain hasn't gotten there yet.

Or perhaps like Daniel it's hard to remember where self-harm and harming others even began. His sister molested him, he molested his younger brother, and porn and drugs and one-night stands, occasionally violent, became a lifestyle. He tried getting married, but an affair and a child with his affair partner soon ended that. He feels irredeemable. Is there any hope?

And then you might identify with Marilyn, who was taken to church from the time she was born. Teen youth group became a place of healthy fun and good friendships—until her youth pastor started showing her special attention. At first her introverted soul felt validated and seen, and the increasing sexual favors seemed a small price to pay. He was her pastor, right? But the web of lies and shame soon cut her off from friends and even from God. She feels like a pile of ugly debris in the corner, not wanting to be seen by anyone, including God.

Honesty. And compassion. That's how we're looking at your story. And it's how Jesus looks at your story too, remember?

So now what? Can there be any such thing as a next step out of this mess? And pray tell, is there any way to deal with this smothering blanket of shame? A full diagnostic workup is in order. The Doctor is in. And we turn to that in the next chapter.

COMING TO FIND YOU

He's here again. Yes, you're in your familiar room, and this isn't the first time you've felt His presence. But this time the only thing you're aware of once you sense His presence is your desire to hide. You feel so, well, naked with Him in the room. Whatever you're wearing feels totally inadequate to shield you from His eyes.

This time He speaks first. *Where are you?*[6]

Oh, if only He hadn't asked that. Doesn't He know where you are? You don't really want Him to know where you are; you'd rather have stayed hidden. He came looking for you, didn't He? You didn't ask Him to come. He's the one who initiated this visit. With a little warning and more time you could have figured out some way to make yourself more presentable. Couldn't He have announced His coming in advance? You would have tried to be better prepared.

But He's asked a question, and it won't do to ignore Him. So you stammer, "I'm sorry I'm so unprepared. I don't like being seen this way. I feel like I'm naked. I'd have preferred some advance warning of Your visit."

He speaks again. You might have expected Him to sound angry, but what you hear sounds more like penetrating honesty saturated with compassion. *Who told you that you were naked?*[7]

What's with all the questions? Doesn't He know everything? And couldn't He ask about something other than about being naked? You might have felt willing to talk about almost anything but that. It's so—shameful. Can't He see that you've worked very hard to cover up? Different attitudes, different behaviors, different labels, different masks. Nothing has worked very well, but it's not like you've ignored the problem. You're trying with all your might to deal with it.

Who told me? Who told me I was not okay, and in need of covering? Okay, you'll try to answer. All those reasons? That just might satisfy Him. So you start explaining all the reasons—all the people who did things to you and all the circumstances that got you into this mess. He wants to know who? You'll tell Him who! It's him, and her, and them, and

70

that institution, and those messages. All kinds of people told you. And all the lies, wounds, and empty places just keep spilling out.

And when you're finished, He speaks once more. *What have you done?*[8]

This is too much. Didn't He just hear you explain it all? Doesn't He care about all the reasons? Okay, so you've done stuff, but you had your reasons.

As you sit there, unable to escape His gaze, you again see in His eyes the unflinching honesty and the inescapable compassion. Feeling more naked than ever, you kind of collapse into a puddle. He's always known the answers to the questions He's asked you. He didn't ask because He needed to know, but because *you* needed to know.

It suddenly dawns on you: He came to find you even knowing all that. And the warmth in His eyes and His open arms seem to say "I love you" in a way your brain actually begins to believe. He loves you—right now! Right in the middle of this mess.

This relationship is going to be more complicated than you anticipated. Well, it feels complicated to you but you sense it's not at all complicated for Him. He doesn't seem stressed at all. He's just here.

Yeah, that's it. He's just here. And He's not going anywhere.

Questions to Discuss or Contemplate

- What's your response to the list of ways intimacy has gone wrong in our world? What would you add to that list?

- Can you see how some of the ways you were sinned against incited some of the ways you've sinned? What do you think of that idea?

- What would it take to win your heart? Who or what have you given your heart to already? How has that served or not served you well?

- What role has shame played in your story, specifically in your sexual story?

4

the haunting:
where you are now

Man never achieves a clear knowledge of himself unless he has first looked upon God's face.

John Calvin, Institutes of the Christian Religion

Everyone has a sexual story that continues to impact them today. Your sex life is not unrelated to how you bring yourself both to the outside world and to your closest personal relationships. If you can't easily see this in yourself, consider some of the people around you.

You might know a young businessman who's always at work driving hard for success. His wife is beautiful, but the rare times you see them together there's little visible affection between them. You could guess they're not having much, if any, sex, and both he and his wife are ripe for having affairs if they haven't already done so.

You might know the middle-aged wife and mother who exudes confidence, humility, and resilience. It's clear she sees herself as a partner with her husband, neither trying to control him nor being controlled by him. She's being cherished at home and it shows in how she carries herself. You can imagine sex between them is mutual and satisfying.

You might also know the awkward college student, the bitter grandparent, or the single neighbor who's truly generous. Married or single, young or old, you can tell a lot about a person's experience of intimacy by how they exude shame, selfishness, fear, or aggression, by whether they're voraciously grasping, hiding behind thick walls, or perhaps self-confident enough to be fully and generously present with others.

Earlier in this book you were invited to look at previous chapters of your sexual story, the things that have gone into making you who you are now, both things that have happened to you and how you've responded, good and bad. We've **How's your** addressed the way you were originally created and **sex life?** the damage evil has done to that original design both in the world at large and in your personal story. Hopefully you've honestly looked at where you've come from and felt some compassion for those earlier versions of yourself.

Now we're going to focus on the chapter you're living today.

During my years of medical practice the first thing usually required in order for me to give appropriate care to a patient was an accurate and complete diagnosis. What symptoms do they have? What's causing those symptoms? And then we addressed how to treat or manage the problem(s).

After caring for thousands of women as an ob-gyn physician, there were many times I could walk into a room and immediately sense at a gut level what was going on. I also learned to trust experienced nurses who spent time at the patient's bedside. When an experienced nurse believes something's wrong, it's smart for me to check it out.

I also saw how a single symptom doesn't always give a complete picture of how serious the medical problem is. If the underlying issue isn't identified and treated, the patient won't get better. Is this headache simply from sleeping in a bad position, or is it a brain tumor? I can treat your fever with Tylenol but that won't help a serious underlying infection, which requires antibiotics.

So how's your sex life? You have one, you know, regardless of your relationship status or whether you're having sex these days or not. And what might the signs and symptoms you display right now be saying about the matters in your heart when it comes to sexuality and intimacy?

Your Body: Friend or Foe?

Humans are embodied beings and you can't address your sexual story fully without considering your body. How do you feel about your body? Ever since the time of Plato, much of humankind has seen the material body as bad, something to be hated and despised. In Platonic philosophy the body is something to escape from. The real you is spiritual and immaterial, and your body is holding you back from your fullest existence.

You might think those last sentences almost describe a New Testament view of the body, but they don't. Platonic dualism, the attempt to demonize the body and elevate the soul, is from pagan philosophy, not the teachings and way of Jesus. The devil's goal is to separate body and soul. As author Christopher West poignantly comments, "There's a fancy theological word for the separation of body and soul. Perhaps you've heard of it: *death*."[1]

Perhaps you feel like the apostle Paul, who seemed to have a love-hate relationship with his body at times. "But I discipline my body and keep it under control, lest after preaching to others

I myself should be disqualified" (1 Corinthians 9:27). "Wretched man that I am! Who will deliver me from this body of death?" (Romans 7:24). But he could also say, "Or do you not know that your body is a temple of the Holy Spirit within you, whom you have from God? You are not your own, for you were bought with a price. So glorify God in your body" (1 Corinthians 6:19–20). Friends, it's not cool to see or treat the temple of the Holy Spirit with contempt.

The incarnation, life, death, bodily resurrection, and ascension of Jesus forever changed the true message about the body. Jesus did not come to free us from our body but to redeem it, along with every other part of His creation. We too often forget how human and physical Jesus was on earth, and still is in glory today. His resurrection did not free Jesus from a physical body. He did not enter an immaterial existence, leaving His body in the tomb—the tomb is empty! His body was changed into a new, glorious, incorruptible body. After His resurrection He ate with His disciples and invited Thomas to touch Him.[2] Our eternal existence will not be as disembodied spirits; those who are saved will have a new, glorious, incorruptible body too.[3]

So again, how do you feel about your body? About the sexual parts of your body?

- Do you hate your body, perhaps for being a focus of lust from another person? Or for becoming aroused when you were sexually molested or abused?
- Do you use your body as a source of sexual power to get attention or validation from others or to exert domination over them?
- Have others' remarks about your body made you see your body as dirty or ugly? Do you treat your body in ways to prevent others from seeing you as a sexual person?

- Is experiencing physical pleasure the driving force in how you interact with the world and with others? Have you idolized your body in some way?
- How are you dealing with your aging body when it doesn't perform or respond sexually or otherwise as you wish?
- Have you tried to split your body and soul apart, excusing how lust drives your behaviors while minimizing the impact of those behaviors on your inner being?
- Do you look at your sexual desires, sex organs, femininity, or masculinity with contempt?

A school psychologist I talked with recently expressed how gender dysphoria is becoming an increasingly large issue, especially for girls right at the time their bodies are going through the changes of puberty. There's more to sexuality, gender, femininity, and masculinity than your body, but the way you see your body affects this greatly.

Isabelle doesn't like living in her body. She struggles to care for her body with appropriate nutrition, rest, and care. She doesn't like to present herself in any way that appears physically attractive, even to her husband. Being seen as attractive has come to mean danger to her.

George desperately wishes to be free from his body. His physical sexual desires, fueled by porn, include both men and women. He wonders why God doesn't answer his repeated prayers to remove his sexual desires completely. Sexually explicit dreams frequently disturb his sleep. He feels enslaved to the sexual impulses in his body, and he hates it.

Take stock of your current relationship with your body. Do you see it as friend or foe? Can you stand in front of a mirror naked and bless each part of your body? What might it mean to fully embrace that your body, all of it, is the temple of the Holy Spirit?

The State of Your Soul

On the walls of my office are the words *It is well with my soul.* What a glorious state to be in. Recently at breakfast I asked a friend, "How's your soul?" I often find myself asking coaching clients, close friends, or others that question. My friend responded, "My heart is closed about some things, and open and expectant about others." In asking that question, I'm not using the term *soul* in the multifaceted scientific neurobiological sense.[4] I'm simply inviting a moment of reflection on how well or not well the person's inner world is doing.

So how's your soul?

Very few of us engage in self-reflection with any regularity. Life is busy. And if you stop long enough to consider the state of your soul you may be afraid the bottomless pit will open and you'll be swallowed alive, sucked into a vortex of emotions impossible to get out of. Thanks, but no thanks. You'd rather keep sewing fig leaves together and working harder to distract yourself with work, noise, and moments of superficial relief.

But sooner or later you discover that you can't outrun the state of your soul. More and more of your energy is diverted to trying to keep the lid on, and it's exhausting. You might be existing, but you're not really living. You're certainly not living fully alive. The pot of angst inside either eats you alive like a house being destroyed by termites or it explodes in a more or less spectacular blaze of anything but glory.

Reflecting on the state of your soul requires addressing feelings. Emotions. That thought might make you want to close this book right now. Feelings are dangerous. The only thing you want to know about feelings is how to dismiss them, how you can develop more willpower to ignore them and do the "right" thing. Feelings have gotten you in trouble, after all. A good follower of Jesus doesn't follow their feelings, right? So don't talk about them or even acknowledge them. Just try harder. (How long can you keep this exhausting pace up?)

> Sooner or later you discover that you can't outrun the state of your soul.

Or emotions might seem to be those ginormous but fuzzy things that rule your moments and your days even as they slip through your fingers like sand. They feel out of control and are often all you're aware of. Anger, sadness, fear, lust, or bitterness keeps swirling in your mind and you feel at its mercy. It's as if "someone else," your feelings, is at the controls of your life. But you rationalize, *That's just my personality. I'm an emotional person.* Perhaps you've even prayed for God to take away your feelings. (Has He?)

In doing my own internal work, I remember when I said to myself, *Everyone in my family is so angry except me. I'm glad I'm not angry like that.* How wrong I was! My view of God and of success meant I needed to cover up my anger as well as any other emotion and just keep doing. Becoming familiar with the full range of my human emotions, including anger, helped me right-size them and take them out of the driver's seat. I could befriend my feelings and be curious about them, and still not follow them as a guide.

Some have described four basic emotional states: mad, sad, glad, and afraid. If you're not used to being aware of or conversant about your emotions, start with a brief inventory of these four basic feelings. On a scale of 1 to 5, how mad/angry am I?

About what? How sad am I? About what? What am I afraid of? Is there anything I'm glad about? When you identify a certain emotion as most "real" for you right now, sit with that for a bit and notice where you feel it in your body. Or use one of the many feeling wheels available. Consider taking an inventory of these emotions for five minutes each evening and even recording it in your journal.

These questions may help you further consider the state of your soul:

- How were emotions dealt with in your family of origin? Are you aware of and able to recognize and talk about your emotions now?
- Do you know how you feel? Does anyone else know how you feel?
- What do you usually do when you experience a strong feeling? Ignore it? Obsess about it? Act on it? Take it out on someone else? How well do you regulate your emotions?
- Is your heart open or closed? Do you feel hopeful and expectant, or despondent and hopeless, about life, about your soul, about the future?
- How full or empty do you feel inside? How are you trying to fill up your empty places?

Deirdre had several sexual relationships prior to getting married. When she and Dale became Christians shortly after they were married, many things changed. But one thing that didn't change was the lust foundation of their sexual relationship. Even though she had a strong sex drive, over time Deirdre came to resent being used and objectified for Dale's pleasure and she began to withdraw from him physically and emotionally. Neither of them was getting their soul filled up.

Lust. It may be the biggest emotional elephant in the room when it comes to sex and sexuality. Don't make the mistake of assuming this is the only or even the most important feeling in your sexual story, but it's often a big one. The biblical idea of lust is not solely or even primarily sexual. James says, "You desire and do not have, so you murder. You covet and cannot obtain, so you fight and quarrel. You do not have, because you do not ask. You ask and do not receive, because you ask wrongly, to spend it on your passions" (James 4:2–3). The King James Version says, "That ye may consume it upon your lusts." It's the idea that *I want what I want when I want it, to do with it as I want for as long as I want for my own pleasure or gratification.*

Lust is not the only emotion you will need to contend with. But consider: What do you want to consume for your own pleasure? If you're married, do you want sex with your spouse mostly for your own gratification? That's lust. If you're not married, are the sexual behaviors you've engaged in focused on your own wants? Jesus is talking about this when He says, "But I say to you that everyone who looks at a woman with lustful intent has already committed adultery with her in his heart" (Matthew 5:28).

Simple appreciation of another individual's appearance is not lust. It can become lust when you allow your heart to sit with a feeling of "I want that for myself." Lusting

> Jesus did not come to squelch eros but to redeem it.

for your spouse is no less sinful than lusting after someone you're not married to. The sexual desire God built within you has been so hijacked by evil that most of us have a difficult time separating sexual desire from lust. An important truth is that Jesus did not come to squelch eros but to redeem it. As Christopher West says, "Salvation begins right here—with the redemption of eros."[5] More on that in chapters to come.

So when it comes to the state of your soul, what role is lust playing?

There are additional emotional dynamics in your soul that can light up like those red flags on the laboratory report of your blood work, showing something is not normal. The point is not that you have difficult emotions. Difficult emotions happen to all of us. They happened to Jesus. To be human is to feel difficult emotions. They become a problem when we allow them to be in the driver's seat or when we try to bury them instead of deal with them.

Anger shows itself frequently when dealing with sexuality. Anger per se is not ungodly, but evil twists and uses anger for its own purposes. Lust breeds entitlement, and together they draw on anger as a fire sucks up oxygen. Mental health counselor, ordained minister, and author Jay Stringer writes, "When masculine anger is sexually hijacked, it moves into degradation of the feminine."[6] George, who we met a few pages back, feels as much shame over his anger as he does over his lust. And he feels just as powerless to do anything about it.

Undealt-with bitterness and a refusal to forgive will sabotage your road to sexual wholeness. You have good reason to feel as you do. You've been hurt sexually, perhaps traumatized in ways beyond words. The trauma responses in your body and your brain may seem to control your life. You might have been told that as a good Christian you must forgive, but you can't seem to let it go. Your pain is real, but when your bitterness becomes a precious thing that you protect and nurture in your soul it begins to destroy you. (Forgiveness is not saying "It's okay." More about the often long process of forgiveness in chapter 7.)

We've just scratched the surface of what may be going on in your internal world. If you haven't done so yet, take some time to ponder, *How's my soul?*

Your Relationship Status

Some would say that the only good thing Facebook has ever done has been to allow the relationship status "It's complicated." And is there ever any relationship status that isn't? We've been talking about the need, desire, and capacity for intimacy that God built within each of us. That means we need relationship. But relationships are frustrating because they involve those pesky things called people. They're messy, always.

It's natural to look to others to fill you up. Maybe you approach the world with the belief that if you can find the right person you will finally be fixed. Developmentally that makes sense; you started out in life totally dependent on others for your very survival. Perhaps now if you can find the right pastor, therapist, friend, spouse, or sexual partner you'll finally be okay. But when you find that sexual partner and you're still not okay, you feel confused. Wasn't this supposed to work? Your personality may lead you to sit back waiting for that person to make you okay, or you may try to wrestle out of them what you need. But either way, you're disappointed.

Peter had always felt a bit different and struggled to feel connected with others even when he was with friends. When he got married in his forties, he was sure his lonely days were over. So when his wife often pulled away from him in bed, it was—complicated. He tried talking to her about it but all she would say was, "You don't know how to love me." The thing he thought would finally fix him, marriage, became the source of even more loneliness.

Sexually, where are you when it comes to your relationship(s)? If you're married, lovemaking with your spouse can trigger mental pictures or feelings from past relationships or from porn, trauma, or other experiences. Being fully present in this moment becomes a challenge, and when you're not fully present your sexual satisfaction is derailed. You might find yourself ashamed for trying to use your spouse, or angry that your spouse isn't responding. Or you might shut down your heart when it seems your spouse is trying to wrestle something out of you that you don't have to give.

If you're not married, what you look for from relationships is colored by your sexual story. You might always be on the hunt, wondering if this might be the one to finally satisfy you. Wanda had been married twice, and divorced twice. She's pretty much given up on marriage but she hasn't given up on trying to find a man to sexually fulfill her. She's become very good at negotiating sexual relationships, but real intimacy continues to elude her regardless of whether she "puts a ring on it" or not.

Much of the Christian church now talks about "relationship with God" more than they talk about denomination or church affiliation. That's a good thing. But that phrase can become overused to the point that we miss what we're really talking about. Your relationship status with God can also feel—and may be—complicated, at least to you. One of the primary ways Scripture talks about our relationship with God is to liken it to the relationship between a lover and a beloved. So it makes sense that your sexual story affects how you see God and how you feel about Him.

In looking with both honesty and compassion at your relationship with God right now, how would you describe it? A helpful gauge can be to listen to what your prayers sound like. If you were navigating your marriage or your relationship with your best friend the same way you are negotiating your relationship with

God, how would that turn out? Many people tell me their prayers are some version of, "Help me. Bless me. Bless my friends and family." How would your friendship or marriage be if your communication sounded like your prayers to God? What if you or they were always only asking for things? Or always complaining? Or never addressed the hard stuff?

Your relationship with God would change if your prayers sounded more like conversations between good friends or healthy partners. Perhaps the reason your relationship with God seems so challenging is a reflection of your lack of learning how to have decent relationships with others. What would that good relationship look like? It would involve both listening well and sharing deeply, both giving and receiving, knowing and being known. You'd talk about superficial things and deep things, good things and hard things. And sometimes you'd just "be" without talking at all. Could your relationship with God look more like that?

What is your relationship status? And by that I'm not asking if you have a ring on your finger. Remember, it's complicated. So, married or unmarried, how has your sexual story worked itself into your relationships right now? Some further questions for self-reflection:

- How are your feelings impacting the relationships with people around you? Do you blame others for how you feel? Do you pretend everything is okay when you're not okay? Do you expect others to "contain" your emotions for you?
- How open or closed is your heart toward those around you? Do you expect harm or disappointment, and so keep your heart closed?
- How might you be prone to using others, including your spouse if married, for your own purposes?

- If you're having sex, how present are you with your partner? Is old stuff distracting your mind? Is sex primarily about you? Is sex primarily about your partner? How mutual is your sexual connection?

- How is your sexuality coloring your friendships? Are you often "on the hunt"? Are you hiding, defensive, or aggressive?

- In your relationship with God what do your prayers sound like? How authentic are you? How close or far away do you imagine God to be when you pray?

Perhaps you feel even more alone after considering the state of your relationships with others and with God. Where to go now?

We've taken the journey down to the bottom and looked around at your current state. Now we begin the climb upward. The choice is yours at each step along the way. This is not a climb of weariness or pressure. It's going to be okay. And you're not alone.

LET'S DEAL WITH THIS

The room feels stuffy. You've got to get some fresh air. A walk will do you good. Isn't exercise supposed to be good for you in many ways? You find yourself walking along a familiar path. The sun feels warm on your back. You know this path is often used by joggers but there's no one around today. That's good. You don't feel like seeing or talking to anyone.

You round a corner and there He is, sitting right where you'd hoped to stop and rest. It's like He knew exactly when you'd be walking this way. But how? This isn't when you usually come here. Yet some small part of you had hoped you might see Him again soon.

He invites you to join Him. You're tired; it couldn't hurt. But why are you tired? You slept okay last night and you haven't walked that far. You realize your tiredness has little to do with your body. You don't so much sit as collapse under the weight of the inner weariness you feel.

Even though part of you had hoped to see Him again, you're not fond of surprises. He wants to talk and you don't have much energy to resist. He sees right through your half-hearted attempts to divert the conversation to religious controversies. Come to think of it, He sees right through all of you. He talks about matters of the heart, and makes you an offer that seems too good to be true. The lies you've come to believe—He desires to exchange them with truth. The wounds you've accumulated—He offers healing. That would be nice. And the empty places in your soul—He wants to fill them up. You can't even imagine really being satisfied.

He might be the best salesman ever but okay, you'll bite. *I don't want to be weary and hurt and empty anymore. Let me have this!* There, you've done it. You've asked. Isn't that what He's wanted? You've said yes.

You might have expected Him to follow through on His promise to give you that satisfaction, to fill up your emptiness immediately. But He seems to pull a bait-and-switch on you. He asks something from you, the very thing you don't have to give. Or at least what you don't want to. With laser precision He puts His finger on that one thing you'd hoped to keep hidden, the part of you that you'd hoped would just go away, the *it*. "This right here," He says, "let's deal with this."[7]

87

You try to protest for a moment but it's no use. Your emptiness is so great and the promise He offers is even greater. Your weariness breaks and you find yourself letting all your internal angst roll out right there in His presence, with the sun warming your back and His gaze warming your heart. Time passes—you're not sure or concerned about how much time. You feel full inside and at the same time haven't a clue what to do next. But for right now, you're not worrying about the past or the future. It's as if this is the first time in a long time, perhaps in forever, that you've been fully present. You feel truly seen and known. You didn't think it possible to be seen and known without having the other person turn away, but you are now. And the very neural circuits in your brain are feeling different.

This journey to addressing the lies, wounds, and empty places inside is not turning out to be simple, and your relationship with Him isn't turning out to be simple either. Well, it may not feel simple, but it's coming down to simple honesty. In spite of that, there's a life in your soul that feels good. Your weariness doesn't matter quite as much. Rest feels possible now.

As wonderful as this moment has been, there's no question it's just the beginning. When He sees you, He sees everything that brought you to this moment, all the junk of your life. He sees the reality of where you are right now, the reality about your body, your emotions, your relationships. But He also sees exactly where He is inviting you to go, the glorious you He is in the process of creating. He sees all of it, past, present, and future.

He gets you. You feel felt, seen, and known. And that feels even warmer than the sun on your back.

Questions to Discuss or Contemplate

· How have you been treating your body, the temple of the Holy Spirit? What would it mean to treat your body with the preciousness a temple would require?

· What is the current state of your soul, especially around sexuality? What role is lust playing? What about anger, shame, loneliness, or bitterness? Any other themes?

· How has your sexual story been impacting your relationships currently? How would you assess your relationships with the one or few people closest to you? How is your relationship with God right now?

· The picture of Jesus putting His finger on that place in your soul and saying, "Here, let's deal with this"—have you sensed that? What is that like for you?

healing is a choice:
embracing the process
of transformation

Kindness is the instrument God uses to open the heart and begin its renovation.

Dan B. Allender, Healing the Wounded Heart

Anita had a complicated sexual story. She'd mostly tried to ignore her sexual story until her two daughters began approaching the age of puberty, and now she felt totally unprepared to help them navigate the accompanying physical, emotional, and relational aspects of growing up. While Anita had never slept with anyone except her husband, the ways she'd learned about sex growing up had been somewhat traumatic. And she'd recently developed the inner strength to say no to aspects of sex with her husband that were harmful and demeaning. While Anita wanted to feel better, she wasn't sure about healing or whether she really wanted to deal with her sexual story. She wrote me, "I need my trauma for my protection. I don't really want to part with it."

Randy had been trying to imagine a life of sexual wholeness but he didn't think he could go there. His marriage was troubled and his wife had explicitly said she wasn't open to considering sex again, ever. She told him, "Go take care of yourself any way you want. I don't care." Randy had struggled with porn off and on for years. It had become a stress reliever even though he felt guilty about it. Now his wife's ultimatum and "permission" made him seriously consider finding a mistress. He wrote, "I can't go the rest of my life never having sex again. God might send me to hell if I go outside my marriage, but it seems like I don't have any other choice."

Both Anita and Randy have a mental picture of what they believe sexual wholeness would look like. Anita imagines it would mean having to say yes to her husband's desires for sex when and how he wanted it, regardless of how traumatic it might be to her. Randy imagines it would mean living under his wife's ultimatum of "no sex" forever and having to stuff his sexual drives with absolutely no outlet. Both imagine sexual wholeness primarily as a matter of dos and don'ts, all about behavior.

If that's what you imagine sexual wholeness to mean, no wonder you feel ambivalent. If that's healing, do you really want it? Just asking the question can feel un-Christian. You feel guilty for not wanting a life controlled by another's demands (either your spouse's or God's), or a life of constant white-knuckling it trying to keep from doing what your body and mind keep screaming for, or wondering if you'll put in all this effort and end up messing up again. Is it really worth it?

I wouldn't want that kind of life, and you shouldn't either.

Perhaps if God would magically rain down healing on you from on high in one wonderful moment you might take it. If He could instantly remove your sexual drives so that you'd never want porn again, okay. Perhaps you've begged Him for that. Or perhaps you've tried to "pray the gay away," pleading with God to change who you're sexually attracted to. But this process of living out the transformation journey feels too hard, too complicated, too messy. Can you even do it? Do you really want to?

So what is Jesus inviting you into? If you choose to say yes, what are you saying yes to? What does healing look like?

Messy Vocabulary

As an author, I pay attention to words. Words matter. And often they're messy, nuanced, or incomplete. It's important to be clear about what we're talking about.

When I first started wrestling with these ideas, I used the phrase "sexual integrity." There's a lot of goodness in that phrase. Integrity has been a value I've sought to live by in every area of my life. One of the best compliments I ever received during my medical training was from a dear professor who wrote on my evaluation, "She does what she says and says what she does." I wasn't sure I deserved that compliment, but that's integrity. Integrity signifies being undivided, living the same regardless of the circumstances or who is watching.

When it comes to sexual matters, however, this phrase has become very focused on behavior. There are many sexual integrity ministries, many who are doing work that is truly excellent and transformative. But what do you think of when you read or hear "sexual integrity"? You might think of staying away from porn, or no sex with anyone except your spouse, or no sex at all if you're single. But as important as those things are, focusing on behavior stops short of bringing you the lasting transformation God has for you. And it doesn't help in integrating what your left brain logically knows with how your right brain subjectively feels.

Randy hears "sexual integrity" and immediately feels hopeless; he imagines that means never ever having a sexual release again. As I've been saying in this book, sex is about more than behavior—it's about matters of the heart. In its full meaning integrity would include matters of the heart, but that's not what most people think of when they hear "sexual integrity."

Sexual healing is another phrase that might be helpful. We've talked about the sexual harm that many, perhaps all, have experienced. Healing was a major part of Jesus' ministry when He was here on earth. There are clearly broken places in your soul that need healing. Jesus offers that!

However, when Anita hears "sexual healing" she imagines it would mean she no longer has a fight/flight/freeze response in her body and mind around certain people, memories, or experiences, and that would mean she would then "have to" have sex with her husband. And she can't imagine doing that without being re-traumatized. Does healing mean you become the "good spouse" the Christian church has implied you're "supposed" to be?

In seeking the right vocabulary I've been using the phrase *sexual wholeness* more and more. I like this phrase the best, even though it also has limitations. It's been used to signify finding freedom from a sexual addiction, but I believe it's a whole lot more than that. Wholeness describes how God created human beings in the beginning. When Jesus was here on earth, He demonstrated what God intended for each of us—body, mind, and soul fully integrated, functioning at our best, deeply connected to other humans and to God Himself. That's the Hebrew concept of shalom: nothing missing, nothing broken.

Do we ever get there in this life?

Perhaps not. In fact, certainly not. But because of Jesus there is an ocean of wholeness available here and now that very few of us take full advantage of. The fact that some followers of Jesus reach amazing degrees of wholeness now should make all of us hungry for more. Be encouraged. Men and women, young and old, married and unmarried have discovered amazing measures of wholeness in sexual matters through the process of transformation that Jesus offers.

You may feel you're too far gone to hope for that. Refuse to believe that lie! If God has done it for others, why not for you? If others have experienced it, why not you?

Let me caution you: When you say yes to sexual wholeness, it will not result in God zapping you from here to there. If you've let the guided reflections at the ends of the previous chapters open your own soul to moments of encounter with Jesus, you realize this is a process. When God does something in a moment, it's wonderful! But He usually works through an ongoing process of transformation.

That process is what you're saying yes to.

Will Anita or Randy ever have satisfying sex with their spouses again? I don't know. Sexual wholeness may look a bit different for each person, and it may not always mean a happy married sex life. What does it look like for me as an unmarried widow? What will it look like for Alice, or George, unmarried individuals we've met before? This is why addressing your individual story and inviting Jesus into your story is so important. For me, pursuing wholeness in this way meant I became capable of having a sexually intimate and satisfying relationship with my husband during our marriage. It means I am not tempted to enter a hotel room alone with a man I'm not married to. It means my experience of singleness now is meaningful, and that I can walk alongside others who are experiencing sexual struggles regardless of their relationship status.

What will sexual wholeness mean for you? God knows. But here are a few things it will certainly mean:

- Your past loses its sting. You will not forget the facts of what happened to you or what you've done. But like Paul in dealing with his history of persecuting Christians,[1] you will not exert energy trying to hide your past. Any trauma becomes "finished" in your brain so that it doesn't feel like it's still happening. You've both offered and received forgiveness where needed.

- Your sexuality becomes integrated. Your trauma or sins or whatever brand(s) of sexual brokenness you've accumulated become integrated into your whole person as scars, not as open wounds. There are no hidden corners in your soul or life that are walled off from yourself, God, or others, even while maintaining appropriate boundaries with people where needed. Sexuality is right-sized in your being and experience.

- Sexual behaviors do not rule you. Whatever addictions you may have had do not rule your daily life any longer. You may have to keep walking the journey of transformation every day, but you are not a slave to any behavior.

- You become capable of intimacy. The walls around your heart come down in appropriate contexts. If married, that includes taking the clothes off your body in ways that bring goodness and connection to both of you. Married or unmarried, you are nurturing deep, healthy, heart-to-heart intimacy with a few others.

How does your soul respond to reading that list? It's certainly an incomplete list, but I truly believe those elements are available to anyone. We'll unpack much of that more deeply in coming chapters. But for now, let your heart dream a little. Notice where you feel the biggest internal resistance. What feels most impossible? Where does your heart scream no? Or perhaps your heart cries, as the woman did to Jesus, "Give me this water!"[2]

It's likely you wouldn't still be reading this book if you didn't feel the pull of the Spirit of God (the Holy Spirit) working in you. The desire you feel for wholeness is His doing. Remember, He is a God of miracles. We've been taught to think of miracles as momentary, and we too often overlook the true transformation God works in those who continue to give Him opportunity. My ability to enjoy a truly intimate marriage in every way after my messed-up past was a miracle. Garry and Melissa Ingraham,[3] who have enjoyed a sexually intimate marriage for over fifteen years after they each had previously lived a homosexual lifestyle, are a miracle. Nick Stumbo, a pastor previously hooked on porn who used his own journey to transform his church, now leads a ministry helping organizations bring healing to others. He is a miracle too.[4] And there are many others.

Why shouldn't your unique miracle be next? Pause even as you're reading this. Check in with God and allow Him to stir a picture in your soul about what sexual wholeness might look like for you. It will be an incomplete picture; God doesn't tell you everything all at once. Be open to it looking different from what you might have imagined at first.

And then say yes to whatever part you can. Your yes might be tentative. You might feel anxious about saying yes. Maybe it's yes just for today. Or yes to reading another page of this book. Or yes to considering the possibility. Or yes to asking more questions. It's whatever yes you can say right now.

Healing Is Like Food

The mental picture of God raining down healing on you as if from on high—it's so appealing. You'd love to bypass the struggle. When God doesn't respond with a zap in answer to your begging and pleading, you may be tempted to wonder what's wrong.

But what if healing is more like eating? God knows you need to eat every day (or most days). He rained down manna from heaven in the wilderness *every day* for the children of Israel, not all at once. Your healing will be something you will need to rely on Him for daily as well.

Jesus said "Your heavenly Father feeds" the birds (Matthew 6:26). But He doesn't do that by dropping food into their beaks. It's the same with us. God makes an infinite variety of physical food available. He makes fish grow in the sea, but He doesn't catch it, bake it, and put it on our plates for dinner. He makes grain grow in the field, but He doesn't harvest it, grind it, bake bread, and hand us sandwiches. He doesn't drip IV nourishment into our veins. You and I are responsible to know when we're hungry, find appropriate food, choose it, and prepare it. And then we must eat it—actually take it into our bodies.

Healing and wholeness are a lot like that. You have to acknowledge your hunger, the places in your soul that are not as you want them to be, that desire something better. Someone who is satisfied to remain where they are isn't in a position to receive the transformation God provides.

Finding and choosing appropriate food may seem like a big challenge. Too often sex itself becomes the "food" you seek. If only your spouse would give you sex, you wouldn't be hungry. If only God wouldn't care who you slept with, perhaps you could find the right "one." Or if only you could find the right substance or activity that would effectively numb you out from your trauma or shame you'd feel less desperate.

But how's that working for you?

God won't force you to choose healing, but He does offer it. There is a unique path to wholeness that He has in mind for you, but there are at least three elements of finding that healing that apply to my own story and to everyone I've talked with about their story:

1. Getting under the surface. This means looking at where you came from, what happened to you, what you did in response, and how all these parts of your story are affecting you now. It's looking at your story, your whole story, with both honesty and compassion.

2. Connecting with others. Oh, ouch! You might rather it be just you and Jesus. But you were wounded in relationship (intimacy gone wrong, remember?), and you will find healing in relationship.

3. Bringing Jesus into your story. When Jesus shows up, things change. It's not a zap, but the process becomes possible with Him around. We've started addressing that already, and now we're going to get very specific about how to let Him behind the walls in your heart.

The last few chapters have addressed the first of these elements, getting under the surface. I hope you've taken the time to explore the earlier chapters of your story and where you are now.

Now we'll explore the other two elements more—connecting with others and with Jesus.

How to Connect with Others

In my work with people this is almost always the most challenging element for them to address.

Morgan had been a follower of Jesus since her teenage years but felt deep shame about her struggle with porn. "That's something guys struggle with, but what's wrong with me that I still fall into that?" And now as a woman over fifty she felt very alone with her struggle. "I've never told anyone, ever, about my porn use. I've talked about my divorce and my addiction to food, but you are the first person I've spoken to about this. It's so embarrassing."

As we unpacked Morgan's story, it wasn't hard to see where she had been sexually harmed as a young girl and how her experience of God had been harmed by how God-talk had been mixed up in that trauma. Morgan was determined to find healing and the transformation Jesus offered. She had been meeting with a small group of other women for quite some time and felt like they knew her, but they didn't know this. "They all have other hang-ups, but none of them struggle with porn." She finally found the courage to tell these safe people about this part of her struggle, and the way they received her seemed to disinfect another layer of her shame. Her struggle with porn didn't disappear in one moment, but having these allies for her journey broke the bondage and Morgan sensed her story moving in a new direction.

Reaching out to others is an important step, but not an easy one. I've heard over and over: "I don't have anyone to talk to about this."

- The thirteen-year-old girl on a Caribbean island who doesn't feel she can tell anyone what happens when she and her older brother share a bed most nights.
- The young pastor in Kenya who struggles with porn and is sure he'll lose his church if anyone knows.
- The husband in Houston who had an affair a few years ago and can't bear the thought of telling anyone.

Whether it's a history of sexual harm, a sexless marriage, a sexual-related addiction or struggle, or some other brand of sexual brokenness, just the thought of telling someone can seem terrifying. It will also be the most powerful thing you can do in choosing healing.

This is the most important part of eating—taking healing into your being. It's not just something you sort of believe in "out there," but something you are embracing and bringing into your soul. I've never met anyone, not one person, struggling with a significant sexual issue who has found lasting and ongoing transformation without connecting deeply with a few other healthy, growing people along the way.

David's struggle with porn began when he was seven years old. His marriage nearly ended when his wife found out, but they successfully went through the long, hard process of restoration. Now porn-free for years, David invests regularly in maintaining his new lifestyle of sexual wholeness. When I asked what advice he would give to someone who feels stuck with some kind of sexual brokenness, he immediately responded, "Find a friend!" He continues to meet weekly with three other guys, and the four of them support, challenge, and encourage each other.

Dr. John Townsend calls it people fuel.[5] Dr. Curt Thompson calls it confessional communities.[6] Find your people. How do you do that? Let me suggest three ways. These ways are not mutually exclusive; Morgan is making use of all three of these paradigms. But considering these separately may help you see one next step you can take.

First, there are already organized communities you can join. One of the best things to ever come out of addiction was the establishment of 12-step groups. Though not perfect, these groups offer places where countless people have found safety, support, and healing. Sex and Love Addicts Anonymous (SLAA) and Survivors of Incest Anonymous (SIA) are two organizations especially applicable to people wrestling with sexual issues. Celebrate Recovery is a biblically-based 12-step program helping people experience "sustainable recovery and healing to our hurts" regardless of what they may struggle with.[7] There are other organizations offering groups with various specific focuses, and it's almost guaranteed there is one or several near you.

Is a small group at your church sufficient? Rarely, at least as they are usually conducted. You may have experienced meeting with a handful of others doing a ten-week book study, or something similar. These types of small groups can be helpful, but they don't usually facilitate the lasting healing and transformation you truly need. They are not set up to let you be truly seen and known. You need a place where it's safe to talk about anything, especially the things you don't want to talk about, where you know people won't talk about you outside the group, and where nobody is trying to "fix" you. With a lot of intention some small groups at church can become that place. Twelve-step programs are usually set up with those elements. Other facilitated therapy groups can offer the same.

A second paradigm is to form your own group. That's what David did, and these four guys have continued meeting together for years. To do this, start by writing down a list of your acquaintances or friends, people who might possibly be "your people." Pray about your list, especially about who God might have you reach out to. While you may not know people personally who have the same struggle as you do in every detail, it is guaranteed (I am 100 percent certain of this!) that some of the people you know have struggles similar to yours. You know people who are struggling with porn, living in a broken marriage, single and struggling with their sexuality, wrestling with a history of abuse, or whatever.

A quick note to men: It can be especially difficult for many men to acknowledge the ways they were sexually harmed. But statistics indicate about one in five men have been sexually abused, and that doesn't include early exposure to porn or other ways you may have been harmed sexually. You *can* find other men who need this connection as much as you do.

Make an appointment for coffee, lunch, or a meet-up at the track, with one person on your list. When you meet, say something like, "God is working on me and I know I need to connect more deeply with a few others. I'm wondering if you might be one of my people. Could I share something with you?" Then share one piece of your story. It doesn't have to be the worst part, just one significant piece. And watch how that person responds. If that person minimizes your struggle, tries to fix you with easy answers, or turns it around and makes it about themselves, they're not one of your people. You're looking for someone who literally or figuratively leans in and says something like, "Oh wow. That sounds really hard. I'd like to hear more." Or they might say, "Me too! Let's talk."

Then do that with the others on your list one by one. You're looking for four to six others who are also interested in, as Dr. Curt

Thompson says, telling their stories more truly. You're gathering your tribe who can commit to meeting regularly to support and pray for and encourage and challenge each other. Maybe you know just one person; start by just telling your story to that one person. And over time, perhaps one of your people knows one or two others.

This is hard, my friends. It's scary. It's not something I do easily myself; it takes work. But there is nothing that will make a bigger difference in your journey to wholeness than this.

The third paradigm of connecting with others is to consider professional help. An expert can provide perspective and support that moves you past roadblocks, facilitates healing from trauma, and shows you how to employ tools for living well. A truly knowledgeable and caring pastor can be a priceless blessing. Just make sure your pastor is a people person with a measure of training and experience in transformation and healing. Other categories include a Christian therapist, trauma therapist, or spiritual director. It could be a wise and godly friend that you already have. Embrace the courage to tell them the truth about where you are. Betty had a wise mother-in-the-Lord who had known her from childhood who became an important source of support and healing in her transformation journey.

Getting professional help does not mean you are weak; it means you are intentionally looking for the food God is making available and choosing to take it into your being. If you're stuck, investing time and possibly money to get good professional help may be life-changing.

Who are your people? Like Frodo and the fellowship of the ring, you need a band of brothers or sisters to walk with you. The fact that finding your people is hard doesn't make it either impossible or unnecessary. Please don't rush past this critical part of your transformation journey; it's one of the most important ways your right brain and left brain become more integrated.

Time, Jesus, and Your Story

Time is a funny thing. We humans live within time and we've never known anything else. As the two-dimensional figures in Flatland[8] cannot imagine a third dimension, we can only dimly imagine a fourth. In his general theory of relativity Einstein powerfully demonstrated the concept of a fourth dimension, time. The concept of time travel has fascinated humans for generations.

Time is not a conundrum or limitation to God. "With the Lord one day is as a thousand years, and a thousand years as one day" (2 Peter 3:8). "Jesus Christ is the same yesterday and today and forever" (Hebrews 13:8). God understands time. He created time, and He created us as human beings within time. Jesus, the second person of the Godhead, experienced time when He was here on earth. But because time is no limitation to God, the past and the future, as we conceive of those concepts, are as real to Him as our today is.

This has wonderful implications for your healing and becoming sexually whole. In important ways, trauma stops your brain from completing its processing. You may feel as though it's still happening. Trauma is recorded in your brain without a clear sense of timestamps. The truth that God is not limited by time and that your brain has not yet applied subjective timestamps to your trauma is a marvelous thing. Jesus entering your story doesn't just mean your story today; it's for yesterday and tomorrow also.

For whatever part of your past seems to keep you stuck, go there in your mind. Find a quiet time when you can reflect and imagine. While it may bring up a little anxiety to do so, you'll know you've hit on the right memory when you can put yourself right in that moment. To your brain, it's happening right now. (If you're struggling with debilitating anxiety or similar mental distress, you may prefer doing this with a professional.)

Then invite Jesus into that moment with you. Intellectually you may already believe He was there, but have you truly experienced Him being with you right then? Picture Him in the room with you when you were sexually abused, after school when your friend first showed you porn, behind the bleachers when you and your boyfriend were making out, sitting on your bed upset when you got that breakup text, in your honeymoon suite when you and your spouse couldn't make it work, walking out of the abortion clinic with you, or sitting next to you as you crouched in shame after being raped. Picture Him right there as you tried to act out on your younger sibling what you'd seen in porn, when you first realized you were sexually attracted to someone of the same sex, when you ran from one sexual relationship to another trying to feel okay.

As you picture Him there with you, how close is He to you? Where exactly is He? What's the look on His face? Is there anything you want to say to Him? Is He saying anything to you? Stay there with Him for a bit.

One caution: Remember that Jesus always meets you with honesty and compassion. If you imagine Him in that moment as disappointed in you, condemning, or angry, you may need to soak in some of the stories of Jesus in the Gospels, or address your picture of God with a trusted and safe friend.

The neurological circuits in your brain begin to change when you feel understood by Him, sensing that He truly gets you. Your brain has an opportunity to finish the story, to complete its processing. This happens as you tell your story more truly to another human being also, but deep and profound healing happens when you experience Jesus being present with you in that overwhelming moment.

Laura worked nights at a truck stop. A recent shooting had triggered her PTSD stemming from a traumatic event one night when she was a teenager. She sat in my living room in a daze describing that night: how a drunk "friend" had shot at her point blank when they stopped along a dark road. She had not been hit, but had always felt no one would have known or cared if she'd been killed that night. As she invited Jesus to be with her in that moment, the look in her eyes changed from trauma to wonder. Instead of feeling God had abandoned her that night, she now saw Jesus standing between her and the shooter deflecting the bullets and saving her life. "He protected me!" The facts had not changed, but their meaning had changed dramatically. Her brain finished the story as she experienced Jesus being with her.

Where in your past do you need to experience Jesus' presence and allow your brain to finish the story? Any memory that still holds power over you can be changed by inviting Jesus to be with you in it. You can do that as often as you need to, over and over again. This is part of choosing healing, of stewarding your sexuality. And it's okay to ask Him all the *why* questions; He welcomes them.

One more thing about God and time. Because He exists outside of time, He not only sees fully all the things that went into you becoming who you are right now, but He sees just as clearly the person He is creating—or better yet *re-creating*—you to be. He doesn't have the angst about speed that we do. It's normal for you to want this healing journey to be done. I remember praying with deep agony, "God, get me through this quickly." He understands those prayers. But He's not worried when our healing seems to take a long time. He also sees the person of glory and wholeness that you will become as He and you continue working together.

SAYING YES

This room has come to feel different. Whenever you come here, you can't help but recall those moments when He's shown up. It never goes exactly as you imagine it will, but you can't deny there's something different not only in this room but also in your soul as a result of His visits. Your heart has begun to imagine a future of goodness. Your mind usually quickly dismisses the thought—that just couldn't be true for you. But the desire has become harder to ignore.

You sit down just for a moment. This feels awkward—starting to hope for something that seems too good to be true. Could He be teasing you? Is this even real?

You're about to get up and leave the room when suddenly here He is again. It doesn't take as long for you to recognize His presence this time. Your ambivalence is still there; He doesn't feel completely safe. But what is "safe" anyway? How would you even know? His eyes catch yours, those eyes that always seem to see more than you're ready for.

"What do you want?" He asks.[9]

Whenever He shows up, He has this way of asking questions that make you nervous. But His words seem to go directly to what your soul had been imagining in spite of yourself: that desire for goodness you'd begun to hope for. It's as if He knew exactly what you were thinking when you sat down.

You don't know quite what to answer. Voicing your desires seems so vulnerable. He seems so righteous, and your desires seem so, well, tainted and small. But He's so appealing. His very presence makes goodness seem possible. Could it be true—for you?

He speaks again. "Do you want to get well?"[10]

Of course you do! Can't He see that? His eyes—they see everything. They see your confusion, how hurt you've been, the shame you've carried, how hard you've tried without success, all the things you've done. Of course you don't want to stay there. Of course you want to get well!

But before you can speak, a thought suddenly occurs to you: What would getting well really mean? You're quite sure it would mean you couldn't hold on to your trauma as an excuse or protection any longer. You'd have to let go of all the ways you'd tried to get filled up. Those ways haven't worked very well, but could you really let them go? Who would you be if you weren't living out of that mess? Would you even be you if you were well?

And would being well be boring? It might feel nice to have some relief. You've felt moments of relief from His previous visits. But that might only last for so long. What about when you don't see Him right here? Could you do this? Would there be enough excitement to replace the other stuff you'd have to leave behind? Would being well be worth it?

One more time He speaks. "For you to get well means I come in."[11]

Oh, this is getting personal. You shouldn't be surprised; His eyes always seem to invite themselves into the deepest parts of your soul. Becoming well isn't going to be some telehealth robotic remote procedure—it's going to mean inviting Him into the deepest parts of you. He's inviting you to invite Him in. He's not forcing Himself in; He'll only come if you invite Him. But it's clear He wants to come in.

He's not going to say anything else. The next move is yours. As He waits for your response, your mind keeps going back to desire. Wasn't that what He asked you? What do you want? As you sit there, your desire seems to become an all-encompassing awareness, as if a tidal wave were sweeping over you. You do want healing. You do want wholeness. You do want to be well. Whatever it takes.

And you hear yourself say just one word.

Yes.

Questions to Discuss or Contemplate

- When you imagine sexual wholeness, what do you imagine that might look like for you?
- How completely do you feel you've examined the roots of your sexual story to this point? Are there areas yet to explore?
- What's the conversation in your head as you imagine deeply connecting with a few other people and letting them see and know you? What one next step might you take toward connecting in this way?
- What moments from your past seem to keep you stuck, where you need to invite Jesus to be with you there?

6

facing the opposition

Secular theories of evil simply don't add up to a valid explanation of human behavior.

John Mark Comer, Live No Lies

Danika was frustrated. She would make a little progress and then suddenly be overwhelmed with pressure to act out again. It felt like something outside of her had taken over her mind and emotions. She'd usually mess up, get embarrassed, and climb back up on the narrow way, and a few weeks later the cycle would repeat itself. "Is it me, my flesh? Or is it a generational spirit passed down from my father?" she asked. There was plenty of bad behavior to be passed down; her father had controlled the household with rage and went on frequent sexual binges. Danika saw many of his struggles mirrored in her own and it scared her. Was her brain faulty? Did she need deliverance?

Spiritual warfare. It's a topic that has frequently divided the Christian church into those who seek to solve every problem by finding and casting out the demon behind it, and those who believe this is only a real issue for those in some third-world country. Some believe we're too enlightened to believe in a devil in the twenty-first century. Others make a career out of demonology

111

and deliverance. What's right? Why should we care? And what difference does this make in dealing with your sexual story?

If all it took to experience sexual wholeness were a few good facts in your left brain and a few pleasing moments sensing God's presence for your right brain, then maybe we wouldn't have to address spiritual warfare. But if you haven't

Your journey to sexual wholeness will be opposed.

sensed it already you soon will: Your journey to sexual wholeness will be opposed. Biblically, you can think of this opposition as the world, the flesh, and the devil. Though that specific phrase isn't used in the New Testament the categories are certainly there.

When it comes to sex, many would agree that our sexualized culture—*the world*—doesn't help. Your sexual story—that fits into the category of *the flesh*, the whole reality of who you are as a human being. And then there's the devil.

Don't worry; we're not going to get into weird theology here. This is not that book. But if your goal is to move away from where you've been stuck and into a lifestyle of sexual wholeness, it's only right to address the roadblocks you can anticipate along the way. And the way to make sense of what almost everyone walking this journey experiences is to acknowledge that your becoming whole will be opposed. By what? By a real and personal embodiment of evil which Scripture calls the devil, Satan, and his kingdom of darkness.

If this topic seems farfetched and imaginary to you, let me encourage you to keep an open mind, suspend disbelief for a minute, and at least consider that there may be something here. If this topic stirs up anxiety and pressure for you, hang in there; the answer is less complicated than you may have been led to believe.

Thinking about Spiritual Warfare

C. S. Lewis said it perhaps better than any other modern writer:

> There are two equal and opposite errors into which our race can fall about the devils. One is to disbelieve in their existence. The other is to believe, and to feel an excessive and unhealthy interest in them. They themselves are equally pleased by both errors, and hail a materialist or a magician with the same delight.[1]

In warfare, an ambush works because you don't know or believe it's coming. Denying the existence of the devil gives him a great advantage in his assault on your wholeness. And just as damaging is being preoccupied with the kingdom of darkness and what the devil is doing. In my own research I've found that those who thought most frequently about Satan and demons causing them problems were significantly more likely to experience anxiety, depression, and generalized psychological distress.[2]

What is a healthy and helpful way to think about this? As with everything, Jesus is our best example. As hard as our lives may be, none of us will ever have Satan and his kingdom of darkness arrayed against us to the degree that Jesus did when He was here on earth. The Jews of His day believed in demons and had developed elaborate rituals to get rid of them. When Jesus shows up, He never goes looking for evil, but whenever it presents itself (as Satan himself or as a demon-possessed human being), Jesus is not ruffled. The only drama comes when the demons resist Jesus' commands. The people around Jesus are astonished. This is unlike anything they have seen from their Jewish teachers or exorcists. "They were all amazed, so that they questioned among themselves, saying, 'What is this? A new teaching with authority! He commands even the unclean spirits, and they obey him'" (Mark 1:27).

No drama. No elaborate rituals. No fear. Just simple authority. And Jesus made it clear that as His followers we have been given that same authority over the kingdom of darkness.[3] No losing sleep. No trying to get strong enough to defeat the devil. (Don't try that; you won't win. And by the way, Jesus already did that!) No frantic gathering of spiritual weapons to go out swashbuckling against evil. Our position as followers of Jesus is to stand—to take your position on God's side and refuse to be moved. That's how you overcome the enemy.[4]

Okay, fine. But what's that got to do with sex?

There was a time early in my Christian walk when I would have told Danika that she needed deliverance. But I've come to understand more of how God works, and what I actually told her was much more nuanced.

Every one of us has been born into a messed-up world. Our very DNA is messed up—physically, emotionally, and spiritually. We grow up in messed-up environments. Our brains develop templates about how to relate to the world based on what we see and experience, and those templates are always incomplete, broken, and sometimes downright toxic. Even if Satan himself were already eliminated you and I would still have our own issues—sexually and otherwise.

As followers of Jesus, we know the end of the story: Jesus wins!

And the devil hasn't been eliminated—yet. As followers of Jesus, we know the end of the story: Jesus wins! But we still live in the middle of the mopping-up operation in the conflict between God's kingdom of light and Satan's kingdom of darkness. We get wounded in the crossfire, some of us more and some of us less, but each one of us is affected by the assault from the enemy of our souls. Our enemy knows very well how to exploit our genetic tendencies, our faulty brain templates, and our history of trauma and pain in getting us increasingly hooked on bad stuff and mired in shame so we stop believing anything else is possible.

Remember chapters 2 and 3? God designed a glorious life for you, a life of goodness and true intimacy. Evil came and messed everything up. Your sexuality is a big part of how you are made in the image of God, so of course that part of you will be especially assaulted. As Christopher West says,

> If we want to know what's most sacred in this world, all we need do is look for what is most violently profaned. The enemy is no dummy. He knows that the body and sex are meant to proclaim the divine mystery. And from his perspective, *this proclamation must be stifled.* Men and women *must be kept from recognizing the mystery of God in their bodies.*[5]

For Danika, and for most of us, the answer is a combination of factors. Yes, your brain is faulty. Your neural networks got messed up a long time ago, long before you knew you were learning any of this stuff. You were harmed, sexually and otherwise. You responded badly, sometimes through inaction, sometimes through ignorance, sometimes through outright rebellion. And your enemy has been hard at work assaulting you right where he knows you're vulnerable. So what you need is "all of the above": brain training, forgiveness, healing, deliverance, and growing up. And most of all you need transformation. God weaves all these strands together in your own individual pathway to wholeness.

Under Attack

Where has your personal journey to sexual wholeness been specifically opposed? You may quicky have an answer to that question, sensing the darkness and evil surrounding your experiences, emotions, and thought processes. Or you may think this doesn't apply to you. It may be helpful to consider three clues, warning lights on your internal dashboard, alerting you that the enemy is trying to mess with you right now. These are signs to become aware of in your own mind and body. They aren't the only ways the enemy works, but they're super common and you will probably relate.

The first signal the enemy is at work is confusion. God does not work through confusion. "For God is not a God of confusion but of peace" (1 Corinthians 14:33). If your heart and mind feel dark, confused, and swirling, the source of that is not God; it's the enemy. You may latch onto the brain pathways that confusion stirs up and "go there" easily even when the enemy isn't doing his dirty work right this minute. But become alert to when your thoughts get increasingly dark and circle the drain, taking you down like quicksand. Recognize the tactics of the enemy, quit trying to figure it out, develop healthy ways to calm your mind, and run into God's presence. (More about that shortly.)

> Where has your personal journey to sexual wholeness been specifically opposed?

The second sign of the enemy's work is condemnation. Oh, don't you love the verse, "There is therefore now no condemnation for those who are in Christ Jesus" (Romans 8:1)? And yet the Holy Spirit is not finished with us yet. We have growing up to do. There's a big difference between condemnation, which is always from the enemy, and conviction from the Holy Spirit. Condemnation draws you downward and chains you to your past. It feels hopeless, dark, and like the end. Conviction draws you upward with hope and light. It feels like the beginning and pulls you forward into transformation. If you're feeling condemned, you can know with absolute certainty that it's not from God. You may need to marinate in some of the many Scripture passages that demonstrate God is *for* you, not against you.

The third clue that you're under spiritual attack is a sense of control and manipulation. Satan has a sinister way of twisting God's concept of authority and turning it into something deadly. In the home this has resulted in domestic violence and the subjection of (usually) women and children to the whims and desires of (usually) men. In the church this has resulted in toxic religion, cults, twisted applications of church discipline, and attempts at "elder" control of minute aspects of people's lives. This includes using God-talk to justify sexual harm. Jesus never delegated to any human being the right to play junior Holy Spirit in anyone else's life. They may or may not be doing it intentionally, but if manipulation and control are in play, you can be certain it's not from God.

If you sense confusion, condemnation, or control and manipulation going on, you know it's from the enemy, whether it's directly from him in the moment or more generally as a result of our sinful, fallen world. Use these feelings as a barometer to alert you that something is wrong, but don't use them as a test of reality. Be especially cautious about making any decisions out of these feelings.[6]

What about specific sexual temptations? Is it a demon of lust, homosexuality, or the like that's after you? Sakir had become a Christian in his teens and his heart was overflowing with love for Jesus. But most nights his sleep was disturbed by dreams in which a woman would forcefully have sex with him. He'd wake up wet, ashamed, and terrified. Were these "normal" wet dreams? Was this a succubus (a female-impersonating demon sexually assaulting a person)? That may sound extreme to you. But I've heard enough such experiences from men and women, from both my country and third-world countries, to believe that succubi and incubi (male-impersonating demons sexually assaulting a person) are real.

That may be one of the more dramatic examples of the enemy using our sexual nature against us in his campaign to steal, kill, and destroy, and we'll talk shortly about how embracing victory in Jesus can bring real freedom. A caution, however: Not everything is spiritual warfare. The enemy is real, but blaming the devil for everything bad doesn't help your daily transformation. (Ultimately he is to blame for everything bad, but there's still your human nature and the messed-up world we live in.) If your primary strategy for finding sexual wholeness is to fight the devil, you will never get there. Remember, it's "all of the above." Deliverance, dealing with the devil directly, has a role. But often even more troublesome are the templates in your own brain, the pathways that need to be rebuilt.

Not everything is spiritual warfare.

And then there's that universal human need we keep coming back to—the need for intimacy. You won't find wholeness without addressing those matters also.

Is there a lust demon? A homosexual demon? A rape demon? A demon keeping husband and wife from enjoying sexual intimacy? Demonology can get confusing very quickly, and may often include human speculation. Remember that when Jesus encountered evil He didn't get worked up at all. Based on the Gospels most such encounters were probably not that dramatic: He "cast out many demons" (Mark 1:34). It was usually just a simple "You, be gone!"

One more universal and primary way the enemy works is with what John Mark Comer refers to, drawing on ancient Greek, as *logismoi*, loosely translated as "thoughts." But these aren't just thoughts; they're "thoughts with a malignant will behind them, a dark, animating force of evil."[7] This might look like conversations in your head that sound like your own voice, lies that have just enough truth to give them plausibility, and thought patterns you've followed for so long you assume they're the truth. One of those lies has become rooted in modern culture so deeply you may not realize it's a lie or that you believe it: "I must have a fulfilling sex life if I am to be whole and happy." Really? (We'll address this more in the next chapter.)

Back to the question this section began with: Where has your own journey to sexual wholeness been specifically opposed? A few categories to think about:

- Where has confusion, condemnation, or control been wielded against you, causing harm that you may have tried to assuage with sexual behaviors or leading you to believe God is not for you?
- Has God-talk been used against you in causing sexual harm? This is one of the most sinister ways the enemy causes damage.
- Have you experienced sexual pressures that seem to come from somewhere beyond you, like there's someone "not you" trying to take over?
- What lies do you continue to struggle with? What un-healed wounds are you carrying that the enemy continues

to exploit? What empty places in your soul leave you vulnerable to his enticements?

Sexual issues aren't the only thing the enemy leverages against you, but they're a big one. So what do you do about it?

Unchained and Standing Strong

We've mentioned two broad categories of opposition you will face in your journey toward sexual wholeness: opposition from outside of you and opposition that comes from inside your own brain. We'll address the first category first.

Marta grew up in a sexually disturbed household. As a teen, she was lured into "modeling" and entered a life of high-end sex trafficking. But jetting to exotic locations and $50,000 shopping sprees couldn't soothe the darkness in her soul or provide her the internal strength to escape her traffickers. She turned to various occult practices in her desperate attempts to find peace but only sank deeper into misery. One day she heard the story of Jesus delivering the man tormented with many demons[8] and said, "I want that! I want Him!" It took a process, but years later, Marta now has a beautiful family and ministers to other trafficked women, telling them about the freedom Jesus offers.

During my own years of life-threatening distress, I knew God had the answer, but nothing I was doing was helping me find it. A friend in the body of Christ helped me learn about pleading the blood of Jesus. I started praying that daily as protection against the dark evil spirits that had been oppressing my soul, and everything started to change. I could begin to hear God's voice for myself. I became able to make decisions and think clearly. God still had a lot of cleaning up to do in me, but life became possible. When I stopped that daily prayer, the darkness started closing in again, and I quickly returned to that practice. For over twenty-five years now I've prayed out loud every single day, "Jesus, I plead Your blood over my life, spirit, soul, and body, for today." And I've never again fallen into that pit of torment even when life has been hard.

That said, let me also add that I don't believe there's magic in any specific words you may say. The point is that on your own you will remain vulnerable to the enemy's attacks. Your only hope for safety is to remain, intentionally and daily, under the protection of Jesus. Through His life, death, and resurrection Jesus gained eternal and complete victory over Satan and his kingdom of evil and darkness. He offers that victory to anyone who chooses to take his or her stand on His side. The enemy cannot stand against His cross, His name, His blood. We do that with our words: "And they have conquered him by the blood of the Lamb and by the word of their testimony" (Revelation 12:11). That's why I pray out loud daily the way that I do.

Your only hope for safety is to remain, intentionally and daily, under the protection of Jesus.

You may choose to do something similar. And for people who are especially troubled sexually at night or in their dreams, I encourage them to pray this way out loud before going to sleep: "Jesus, I plead Your blood over my life for this night. I pray that nothing come and affect me this night except that which comes through Your blood. May even my dreams be covered in Your blood." Praying this way does not mean you will never meet deep and real challenges, or that you will not be tempted, or that the other elements of growing in sexual wholeness are not vital. But by taking your stand clearly on God's side daily like this you will not be in bondage to the kingdom of darkness.

That's how to think about the opposition coming from outside yourself. Now, what about the opposition you face from within? Let me suggest three important categories here to keep you from being your own worst enemy: stay clean, stay connected, and stay consecrated.

Stay clean, stay connected, and stay consecrated.

We live in a dirty world. I don't mean that sex is dirty, not at all. Recall our premise that God created you as a sexual being. Evil has marred and distorted what God intended sex and intimacy to be. Cultural norms, popular media, and the countless examples you've seen and experienced barrage your mind and almost unconsciously deepen the ruts in your brain that run back toward sexual beliefs or behaviors that are anything but whole.

Your past leaves you with certain vulnerabilities that are unique to you. Preston had been deeply involved in the sex and drugs prominent in the New York neighborhood where he grew up. He moved away, God radically saved him, and he became an effective evangelist for the gospel. Even decades later he told a group of fellow Christian leaders, "I will never, as long as I live, physically go back to that neighborhood." He knew his vulnerability, and the boundaries God had uniquely placed on him in order for him to remain clean and whole.

There may be things others can do that you cannot do if you truly desire a life of sexual wholeness. That's not weakness; that's honesty and following Jesus. Some refuse to be alone in a hotel room without their spouse or a travel buddy. Some permanently get off social media. Some have a "dumb" phone only (no apps, calling and text only). Some can't watch certain television shows, concerts, or movies, or go to certain places. You may need to make decisions that could seem like a sacrifice but are necessary for your protection. You may have to say no to certain things in order to stay clean. What messages from media, lifestyle, or people make you vulnerable to old brain pathways leading to sexual darkness? That will help you know where to set up some boundaries. Think about activities, technologies, places, situations, or people that you need to say no to, perhaps even permanently, in order to keep your soul clean.

Saying no to certain things is not simply "trying harder"; it's setting yourself up for success. It's valuing the life of growing in sexual wholeness enough to do what it takes.

The second category of dealing with the opposition from inside you is to stay connected. We talked in the last chapter about finding your people, those who you intentionally connect with who know your struggle and can challenge, support, and encourage you. That's not only a critical element in disinfecting the shame of your story and finding a life of growing wholeness; it will be just as important for the rest of your life. Others around you cannot do your fighting or growing for you, but they can alert you to dangers you might be oblivious to on your own. They can provide insight and perspective when you're struggling, and you will also be encouraged as you experience them receiving support from you.

Society has recognized the importance of not facing danger alone. First responders such as police almost always go with a partner. Soldiers don't go into battle alone. Jesus sent out His disciples in pairs.[9] You need a few others who see and know you and are up in your business. It's one of your best protections against the opposition both from outside you and also from within.

And third, stay consecrated. Consecration isn't a word we use much today. Imagine having your own car, you're the only one with the keys, and you can use it anytime you want. You take care of it well, and you might feel proud of it and show it off to your friends. It would feel very different if the car belonged to several people who could each use it as they wished. You wouldn't have the same pride in taking care of it. If the car is yours alone, it's consecrated to you. It's yours.

That's what it means to be consecrated to Jesus. You belong to Him. You are exclusively His. You may have said yes to Jesus' offer of salvation, but have you made Him the Lord of your life? Are you holding on to ownership of your own body and sexuality, or have you asked Jesus to be in charge? You might say, "Of course I've decided to follow Jesus. That's why I'm trying to do this right." You might also wonder, *If Jesus was truly Lord of my sexuality, I'm not sure I could handle it. That might mean I can't do things I want to do or have to do things I don't want to. I'm not sure Jesus is safe enough for me to trust Him as Lord. He might even punish me.* That is ambivalence again, about how your right brain feels about God.

Jesus will never force you. Control and manipulation are the enemy's tactic, not God's. But Jesus does invite you to make Him the Lord of every part of your life. If He is Lord of your sex life, that part of you belongs to Him. Your stance is no longer trying to force yourself to do or not do something. Now you are allowing Him to make His home in you. You learn to listen to His voice and follow Him.

That may sound a bit other-worldly and mystical, but based on the New Testament that's exactly the kind of life Jesus is inviting you into. The cry of the early followers of the Way (what Christians were called before they were called Christians) was, "Jesus is Lord!" This is a big part of inviting Jesus into your story at every moment of the journey. You can pray, *Jesus, I choose You* to be the Lord of my life. I specifically make You the Lord of my sex life. I consecrate my sexuality to You. I purpose to follow You, not by trying harder on my own but by making my body, mind, and soul daily available for You to do Your good work in me from the inside out. You might consider praying this out loud every day as part of staying connected with Jesus in beginning to write new chapters of your sexual story.

HE FIGHTS FOR ME!

It's been a hard day. You're not sure when it started, but you're tired and upset. Nothing has gone well. Nobody has understood you. Your efforts in any direction have fallen flat or come back to bite you. It seems you have no strength left to fight.

And what's the use of fighting anyway? It's too much. The people, the circumstances, the thoughts—everything's dark and confusing. When you try to figure it out, your head hurts. It's as if this unseen force is against you. Every time you try to escape, the opposition becomes stronger. Should you be scared? Should you just give up? Nothing makes sense.

Where did that bit of peace and hope you felt disappear to? When He was last here, you were hardly aware of any outside circumstances. You even lost awareness of your own internal wrangling. When He was here, His presence seemed to take up all the space in the room, in your mind, in your world.

Another wave of darkness seems about to take you out as you utter the only word that seems possible: *Jesus! Jesus!*

Oh wow. It's as if you can suddenly see things you couldn't see before. The darkness feels darker and even personal. If you thought you should have felt scared before, this looks even more terrifying. The darkness seems pointed directly at you, and in the face of it you feel smaller and weaker than you've ever felt in your life.

But you feel no fear. None at all. With a different kind of vision, you have a sense of—Him. You recognize His face but you've never seen Him like this. There's a brightness, a fierceness, a majesty about His presence and a look in His eyes that takes your breath away. There's no mistaking He's King—of everything. King of the room, the block, the city, the world. King of time, of things seen and unseen, of the past, present, and future. King over the darkness. Conqueror over the darkness. And He's standing between you and the darkness.

Oh right, the darkness. Wasn't it about to take you out? Where is it? It's gone, you don't care where. Your nervous system is overwhelmed and you collapse in a heap.

What just happened? Your brain isn't even forming thoughts; you just *are*. The next thing you're conscious of is a hand on your shoulder. As your awareness gathers itself, you open your eyes and see Him looking kindly into you as you've come to expect. It's still Him, but there's no fierceness directed toward you, only warm invitation.

It will take some time for your nervous system to process this. Now that your brain is starting to work again the thought keeps coming, *He fights for me. HE FIGHTS FOR ME!*

You decide you never want to be separated from Him again.

Questions to Discuss or Contemplate

· Where have you felt your journey to sexual wholeness
  being opposed? Where has your story been impacted
  directly by Satan and his kingdom of darkness?

· Have you sensed confusion, condemnation, or control/
  manipulation messing with your mind? How might
  things change if you recognize these as tactics of the
  enemy?

· Stay clean. Stay connected. Stay consecrated. Which of
  these is the biggest issue for you right now? What is a
  step you might take in addressing that?

· Have you ever experienced Jesus fighting for you? What
  might that mean for your experience of dealing with the
  opposition to your wholeness?

toward restoration:
the journey home

The whole life of the good Christian is a holy longing.... That
is our life, to be trained by longing.

Saint Augustine

The moon was the only light as I climbed the hill behind my parents' house. I'd walk up there often after my college homework was done, trying to clear my young adult mind and make sense of my troubled world. God was supposed to feel close out there in the quiet, but He didn't feel close at all. I remember crying out many times, "I can't figure out what's Your part and what's my part. Just tell me what to do and I'll do it." I was trying. I really was.

And my distress only got worse. It would be years before I could understand enough of how God works to effectively cooperate with Him in His transformation of me from the inside out.

Perhaps you have the same struggle. You believe, or at least part of you believes, that God has the answer and that He can change you. Isn't that what happens when you say yes to Jesus? "Therefore, if anyone is in Christ, he is a new creation. The old has passed away; behold, the new has come" (2 Corinthians 5:17). Then why don't you feel new? Why isn't God answering your prayers to heal your trauma, remove your addiction, fix your marriage, or keep you from continually ending up in bad relationships?

And you fall back into the pattern of either trying harder and wearing yourself out, or giving up.

During my graduate studies I came across a body of research that shed some wonderful light on what I had by then been experiencing in my own life and what so many others also experience. As people with some measure of faith, when we face hard things there are three primary ways in which we bring our faith to bear on those problems. Researchers have described three basic styles of what is called religious coping.[1] The first style is self-directing, which says *I may believe in God but I see myself as responsible for figuring it out and making it happen.* The second style is deferring, which says *I mostly sit back and wait for parents, spouse, church, government, even God, to "fix" me.* The third style is collaborative, which says *I see myself as working together with God in addressing whatever issues I'm facing.* Research shows that most of the time those who face their problems with a collaborative style come through challenges with greater physical and emotional wellbeing and greater spiritual resilience.

Collaborative religious coping sounds a lot like Paul: "Therefore, my beloved, as you have always obeyed, so now, not only as in my presence but much more in my absence, work out your own salvation with fear and trembling, for it is God who works in you, both to will and to work for his good pleasure" (Philippians 2:12–13). God works. And we work. He won't do it without us, and we can't do it without Him. It's you and Him working together.

The practical things we talk about in this chapter are ways of doing just that. One danger is that you use these steps as tricks or hacks in simply trying harder. If so, that will only last a little while and you'll fall apart again. That would be self-directing. Another danger is that you skip over these practical steps and simply pray more. That would be deferring. These steps are important, but they do not "fix" you in and of themselves. They are ways you raise your sails to catch the wind of the Spirit.

Have you ever been on a sailboat? I have, once, and it was an awesome experience. We were moving across the water fast, but we were doing nothing to make the boat move. No one was rowing. There was no sound of a motor. And yet we would not have moved at all if we had not raised the sails to catch the wind.

Remember Nicodemus? He was the Jewish ruler who visited Jesus at night so no one else would see him. Jesus told Nicodemus he must be born again. Then Jesus said, "The wind blows where it wishes, and you hear its sound, but you do not know where it comes from or where it goes. So it is with everyone who is born of the Spirit" (John 3:8). The Spirit provides the power for change. He changes you from the inside out. Your job is to raise your sails to catch the wind of the Spirit.

That's what I wish I had understood while out on the hill at night as a college student. This section will show you how to raise your sails to cooperate with God in the process of becoming the healed, whole, and transformed person you were always intended to be.

Being a Friend to Your Body

Your body is not the essence of who you are, but you are not separate from your body. Your body is where you feel the effects of trauma. Your body must be "online" for you to truly be present in your relationships. Your brain's ability to function well is altered by the simple biological processes you either fight against or attend to with care. To become a whole person, someone who is sexually integrated and living with sexual wholeness, you must be a friend to your body.

That idea has become twisted in our contemporary culture, as evil has done with everything. If your body becomes a god, you'll end up chasing every physical sensation and desire. You don't feel like exercising, so you're a couch potato. Or you get addicted to runner's high and push your body beyond the point of wisdom. Or you ignore signals from your body that it needs rest. You believe a sexual impulse means you've got to act on it, now.

Your body is worth listening to and caring for. But your body makes a very unreliable and destructive guide or god. The New Testament views your body as the temple of the Holy Spirit. Think of it: God the Holy Spirit makes His home in your body! And Paul puts this idea squarely in the context of sexuality.

> Flee from sexual immorality. Every other sin a person commits is outside the body, but the sexually immoral person sins against his own body. Or do you not know that your body is a temple of the Holy Spirit within you, whom you have from God? You are not your own, for you were bought with a price. So glorify God in your body.
>
> 1 Corinthians 6:18–20

Juanita wanted to feel closer to her husband. He was a good man for the most part, and their marriage had many good elements. But three children and a full-time job kept her tired and she had little energy left over for either sex or connecting emotionally. As Juanita learned to be a better friend to her body, things improved. She chose to say no to extra responsibilities at work and to some of the extras her children wanted so she could get more regular sleep and find a couple hours each week to nourish her own soul. Now, when her husband invited her to a sexual encounter, her body responded with more pleasure and her mind could be more present. Physical, emotional, and spiritual intimacy became more possible and more meaningful. She even sometimes found herself initiating sex.

If you've been part of a 12-step program you've heard of HALT: don't get too Hungry, Angry, Lonely, or Tired. That's when you're at risk of slipping. If one of your areas of vulnerability is sexually acting out, this definitely applies to you. Being a friend to your body means you decide how to care for it with appropriate food, exercise, and rest. Doing so will dramatically improve your resilience in standing against temptation and building new pathways in your brain in the journey toward sexual wholeness.

Regardless of what your sexual struggle may be, being a friend to your body will move you toward wholeness. The basics matter: healthy nutrition, regular exercise, and consistent rest. It means becoming more aware of the signals your body gives, of when you need to HALT, and what your body needs. Your body is not in charge—you are. But you are paying attention and caring for your body with the kind of care you might offer a friend.

And that idea of the Holy Spirit making His temple in your body? How does that change things for you? It certainly means you don't view your body with self-contempt. Your needs and desires, including your sexual drives, are part of the package. How would you care for and "use" your body knowing the Holy Spirit is living in you?

So what kind of a friend have you been to your body? A few things to consider:

- How are you doing with the basics? How consistently is your body getting the appropriate food, exercise, and rest it needs? What adjustments would be helpful?

- Are you paying attention to the messages your body is sending you? How often do you find yourself blindly giving in to any physical impulse? What would it look like to see yourself as listening to and lovingly but firmly leading your body?
- How do you believe God sees your body? Have you asked Him how He would like you to care for the temple in which He lives—your body?

Learning to Feed Yourself

Your body needs food, and so does your soul. When you were an infant, someone else prepared food your little body could process and brought it to your mouth. But as you grew, you were eager to learn to feed yourself. I'm "Auntie Carol" to my friends' little girl who's almost two. At lunch together recently she wouldn't let me or anyone else feed her. She insisted on using her own little fingers to pick up the sweet potato fries, bits of chicken, and cut-up grapes and put them in her mouth.

Your soul needs nourishment too. We talked in chapter 5 about how healing is somewhat like eating. God makes it available, but you must choose to actually take it into your being. It's the same with the nourishment your soul needs. You don't create food out of thin air. Like physical food, some mental/emotional/spiritual food is healthier than others, tastes better than others, and is easier to find and prepare than others. But you're responsible for knowing when your soul is hungry, finding appropriate nourishment, and actually "eating"—taking it into your being so your soul can metabolize it.

Violet was engaged to be married—for the eighth time. She was embarrassed by that number, and very few people knew how many times it had been. Most of her engagements had led to marriage, but it never lasted long. We talked together about the empty places in her soul and what she really wanted. Her story held plenty of trauma, enough to set anyone up for troubled brain pathways and emotional turmoil. She couldn't seem to stay away from having sex, and getting married made it seem more legitimate. But she had begun to notice

> **Your soul needs nourishment too.**

how unsatisfied she was with sex whether married or not. I asked her, "What are you hungry for? What are you really seeking?"

Roman found himself on a Zoom call with me at his wife's insistence. For months she'd suspected he was having an affair and he finally admitted it a couple weeks prior. He knew it was wrong but couldn't answer why he'd gone that far. Certainly his porn use had disturbed his expectations around sex, but that didn't explain everything. Without trying to excuse his behavior we explored the empty places still unaddressed in his soul. His marriage had been one of convenience for years. There was precious little sex between him and his wife, and when it did happen there was no real connection. That made him vulnerable when a trainer at the gym offered him a chance to be seen and known in a way he hadn't experienced with his wife in years.

Both Violet and Roman were starving. But being hungry doesn't mean that eating poison won't hurt you; lack of intimacy doesn't in any way excuse bad behavior. Understanding the unsatisfied hungers in your soul will help you know what to do next.

Two questions will help you sort this out. First, where are you hungry? What are you looking for when you want sex (or porn or something similar)? You're likely seeking much more than a physical release. You might be seeking affection, validation, connection, emotional intimacy, comfort, excitement, fun, to be wanted, etc. But now you're learning to feed yourself. You can't blame any behavior on the fact that you don't have a spouse, or that your spouse isn't fulfilling your needs. You're the one responsible for understanding your hungers and finding healthy ways to address them. Name your hungers.

The second question is, when have you felt fully alive? What fills you up? It might have been an experience with a friend as a child, or a moment on the beach with the salt wind in your hair. It might have been at a concert, cooking your favorite meal, coffee with a friend, or sitting by the fire with a book and your favorite beverage. What are the elements that have nourished your soul in the past? And how can you do more of that?

Learning to feed yourself decreases your vulnerability to expecting sex to fill you up in a way sex was never intended to. And it will help you pursue intimacy in healthy ways regardless of your relationship status. We'll talk specifically about this in the next couple chapters.

All the other nourishment your soul needs varies depending on your personality, but God created you such that your deepest needs cannot be fully satisfied without a connection with the Person of God Himself. Only He can truly fill you up. Like physical food, you need this connection with God daily. But too many Christians feel discouraged when their daily "quiet time" seems empty and meaningless. God never intended our spiritual nourishment to be boring or one-size-fits-all. As John Eldredge expresses,

> Time with God each day is not about academic study or getting through a certain amount of Scripture or any of that. It's about connecting with God. We've got to keep those lines of communication open, so use whatever helps. Sometimes I'll listen to music;

other times I'll read Scripture or a passage from a book; often I will journal; maybe I'll go for a run; then there are days when all I need is silence and solitude and the rising sun. The point is simply to do *whatever brings me back to my heart and the heart of God.*[2]

How are you learning to feed yourself? What nourishment do you most need that you haven't been getting?

The Matter of Forgiveness

At some point, perhaps at many points, in your journey toward sexual wholeness you will have to face the matter of forgiveness. You've been wounded. You've wounded others. But forgiveness is hard. And it's often been misunderstood. Many people believe forgiveness means something like, "It's okay. It didn't really matter." But it *did* matter! That's why forgiveness is the only way to be set free.

Forgiveness starts with embracing the full impact of the harm you encountered in your sexual story. Your uncle or your mother abused you, or showed you porn. Your youth pastor, music teacher, or athletic coach sexualized their relationship with you. Your first girlfriend ruthlessly shamed you for your sexual naïveté. Your parents shut you down when you tried to ask questions. Your husband used Scripture as a weapon to demand demeaning sex. Your brain needs to wrestle with *This happened to me, and this is how I was affected.*

The harm you've done to others requires forgiveness too. It's hard to look at this without embracing the mountain of shame the enemy loves to heap on you. But remember, you didn't wake up one day and logically decide to harm someone. But you did harm them. If you are in relationship with that person, it can help to ask, "How did my behavior impact you?" No minimizing or shifting blame, just hearing the impact of what transpired.

The path to forgiveness then involves deciding to let it go. Feelings of forgiveness may take longer to catch up to your decision. You are making the conscious choice to release the other person from what they did. You look at the dagger in your soul, take it out, and instead of then using it to stab the one who harmed you, you hand the dagger to Jesus.[3] You walk away from what that person did and choose to not let it continue to wound you. Healing is a yet-to-come step in the process, but that can't begin until you choose to release your grip.

There's a critically important distinction between forgiveness and trust. You can forgive someone regardless of whether they acknowledge the harm or are even still alive. Forgiveness depends only on you—and God. Trust, reengaging in a relationship with the one who harmed you, requires both parties to do their own work. And it requires some measure of evidence that the future might be different from the past. Forgiveness does not require you to place yourself in a position to be harmed again. You can forgive someone without trusting them again. Trust is about the future, and it's a different decision than the choice to forgive.

> I wish for you the freedom of forgiveness.

Seeking forgiveness from those you may have harmed is painful also. They may or may not be willing, right now, to extend you that forgiveness. What you can do is own your role in the harm, apologize without excuse, and with deep humility say, "I was wrong. Will you forgive me?" Trying to force the other person to respond in kind won't work. Asking for forgiveness in many ways places you at their mercy. You may need to walk away and give them time.

Then there's the internal experience of forgiveness. At seventeen Freda became sexually involved with her boyfriend and had her heart broken. For the next several years her sexual promiscuity was legendary among her friends. Becoming a Christian, getting married, and having children changed her life. But Freda's ongoing guilt and shame from her early sexual behaviors was hampering her ability to be intimately present with her husband. We worked together helping her imagine Jesus being right with her when she'd lost her father as a child, when she'd sought solace in the arms of her boyfriend, when she'd used sex to try to fill her empty soul. Over time Freda moved from intellectually believing she was forgiven to feeling in her soul completely forgiven by God. Her left brain and right brain became more integrated, and her connection with her husband, both emotionally and physically, became much more enjoyable.

Feeling forgiven or feeling that you've forgiven someone who hurt you is a process. It's okay to take time with this, and when the wounds are deep sometimes you need to revisit forgiveness repeatedly. You can say, "I'm making the decision to let it go even though I don't feel it. I'm choosing to believe God forgives me even though I don't yet feel forgiven. And I will be honest about my feelings as I keep walking."

I wish for you the freedom of forgiveness.

Escape Plans and Slips

Whatever your personal brand of sexual "stuff," it's absolutely certain you will be tempted again. The process of transformation Jesus takes you through doesn't happen in a moment. Your brain has developed deep ruts that it easily falls into whenever you're triggered, which can be anything from a comment from a friend or your spouse, to something in popular media, to just a frustrating day.

New brain pathways develop slowly. New brain cells grow and develop new connections by about two millimeters a day. That's slow. So when you feel frustrated at your slow progress, remind yourself: two millimeters a day. You're stewarding your sexuality—tending with care to the physical, emotional, and spiritual aspects of how God made you in this deep aspect of your being.

But what you do in the meantime makes a world of difference. One key is to develop your escape plan—what you will *do* when you feel the urge to respond with your old templates rather than as the new person God is creating you to be. God has not promised that you won't be tempted, either directly by the enemy or by the templates in your own mind. But there's always a way out.

> No temptation has overtaken you that is not common to man. God is faithful, and he will not let you be tempted beyond your ability, but with the temptation he will also provide the way of escape, that you may be able to endure it.
>
> 1 Corinthians 10:13

You get to decide what your escape plan is. It is not begging and pleading for God to remove the temptation. Don't stop praying! But an escape plan is what you will *do* at that moment.

How do you build your escape plan? The most effective escape plans target your first step down that slippery slope. Think back to your triggers. The last time you slipped, what was the first moment you can identify that, retrospectively, could have predicted your failure? It may be HALT—you weren't in tune to being hungry, angry, lonely, or tired. It may be a Friday night without anything planned, or a bad day at work, or your spouse's no to sex, or feeling overwhelmed with too much to do, or boredom, insomnia, or something else. Try to see as clearly as you can what the very first element was in the chain of events. Begin crafting your escape plan from that very first trigger.

What could you *do* at that moment that would shift the chain of events in a different direction? You might call or text a friend, clean the house, remove yourself to the bathroom for some deep breathing, recite Scripture out loud, go for a run, read a book that deeply engages you, listen to music you love, walk outside and cry out to God, journal, cook something you love to eat, build a fire in the fireplace, go to a 12-step meeting, watch the birds and look at the flowers, dig in your garden. You get the idea. There are hundreds of possibilities for your escape plan. This is another way you're learning to feed yourself.

Your temptation might be something internal or external. It might be to withdraw from your spouse, fantasize about sex with someone you're not married to, watch porn, or visit a hook-up club. Being tempted is not sin; letting it roll around in your mind or taking action on it is. You can become increasingly alert to the first signs of temptation and develop increasingly strong brain templates that go in a different direction. Your escape plan needs to be actions you take that point your brain in the new direction while your new templates are growing (at two millimeters a day).

A friend is an essential part of your escape plan. The need for intimacy God built within you—that evil has hijacked—requires you to tend to that need for connection. We've talked about this a couple times already, and it's vitally important here as well. There are people you know who are struggling in somewhat similar ways as you are. Do the hard work to find your people and meet with them regularly. And then ask one or more of them for permission to text or call anytime you need to. Offer the same to them.

Should your spouse be part of your escape plan? Perhaps. If your spouse is mature, graceful, and eager to help, sometimes they can be. You're on a business trip, tired and lonely. "Honey, I'm not in a great place. Can I hear your voice for a minute?" Many marriages aren't in a place where that's reasonable. It's so easy for your spouse to take things personally, and it may be hard for them to fully understand. Even if your spouse is one part of your escape plan, you cannot expect them to "contain" your feelings. And you will also need to connect with one or a few others beyond your marriage for this kind of emotional support.

Another element of your escape plan is choosing the thoughts you will think. The lies from the enemy that sound very much like your own voice point you down the road to destruction. "If I don't have sex today, I'll blow up." "I've messed up so many times, I might as well do it again." Choose a mental message you can go back to repeatedly that will replace the lies. Write it on a card to carry with you. Put it as the screensaver on your phone. Rehearse it hundreds, thousands of times. You get to choose what that thought is, but here are a few starters:

- One hour, one day at a time. I can do this today with God's help.
- The Holy Spirit lives in me. I'm not just trying harder; I'm following His lead.
- I have choices. I have an escape plan. I can put my plan into action right now.
- I may feel alone, but that's not true. Jesus is with me. And I have a friend I can call.

But what happens if you slip? Slips are common. That doesn't make them okay. A slip is not a relapse; a slip is a temporary speedbump in your journey to sexual wholeness, but it doesn't take you back to the beginning. Your first instinct may be to embrace the shame again. Don't go there. It's the enemy who immediately shows up to heap shame on you. I'm not sure where I saw this, but it fits: "Religion says, 'I messed up. My dad is going to kill me!' The gospel says, 'I messed up. I better call Dad.'" Run *to* Jesus when you slip, not away from Him. Run to Him as fast as you can. He will never turn you away. Never.

By examining a slip, you can learn a great deal to help your forward progress. Look back at the first steps in your slide downward. What could have been your first clue? You'll probably need to adjust your escape plan as a result. The best escape plan helps keep you from getting into that downward spiral in the first place. How are you going to keep from becoming HALT— too hungry, angry, lonely, or tired? You do it by becoming a friend to your body, learning to feed yourself, and proactively nurturing deep connections with people (even if messy) and a deepening connection with God.

SIN NO MORE

You've been here many times. It's not a place you're proud of. You rarely, if ever, mention this place. You thought perhaps last time would be your last time. You'll try harder next time. But next time has again become this time. The internal pressure, the triggers, the old routines, life—it all leads to this place.

And then the voices begin. Oh, the voices. Old voices, new voices, sneering voices, enticing voices, dark voices.

You're not entirely sure whether it's your ears or your brain that is hearing so many voices. Your brain, yes, some of the voices are coming from inside you. *You'll never be able to stop. This is just who you are. It's not that bad; you have real needs. You can cover this up; nobody will know. Live it up! You're pathetic; it's no use to even try.*

Your mind is picking up speed as it slides toward the familiar dark hole—how far will you slide this time? The voices are deafening and about to crush you.

Then you see Him, here again. How did He know you were on the edge? All the voices pause, as if waiting for Him to speak. His eyes are as piercing as always and His voice breaks the momentary silence: "I don't condemn you."

The silence of the voices lets you breathe. How long has it been since you could even form a thought without the voices screaming? No condemnation. . . . Is this what it feels like to have a clear mind? You're not sure what to do or say. You're just here, still and quiet.

Then He speaks again: "Now let's go and sin no more."[4]

Sin no more? Have You ever tried to "sin no more"? Do You know how hard that is? That's what I've been trying to do, and it hasn't worked! I've worn myself out trying to sin no more. And when I try, the voices always come back louder. The internal pressures, the triggers, the old routines, life—it all just leads me back to that place. How can You expect me to sin no more?

You risk looking up at Him. His look is an invitation. He's not sending you out by yourself to do or not do something, to try harder once again. It's as if His hand is reaching out, inviting you to take it. This isn't going to be just you trying something on your own. And it's not going to be you sitting back and waiting for whatever He might or might not do. It's going to be you and Him doing this together.

Being here with Him makes it seem possible to sin no more. You're not sure what that might involve, but by Him being with you, anything can happen. This working together might actually work!

You reach out your hand to take His. How could He ever want to walk with someone like you? But He does. It might be messy and uncertain, but you know without a doubt that this is the only way to get where your heart most deeply desires—needs—to go.

You will keep showing up. You will keep saying yes. You're all in, fully engaged.

And so is He.

Questions to Discuss or Contemplate

- What are the hungers around matters of the heart that most frequently trip you up? What are some healthy ways to feed yourself in addressing those hungers?
- What does forgiveness mean to you? Are you wrestling with forgiving someone who hurt you? Or in embracing forgiveness for something you've done?
- Take some time to write out your escape plan. Include at least these three elements:
  - ◊ What will be your go-to mental message you will rehearse?
  - ◊ What physical actions will you do when tempted (one or more actions that will involve your physical body)?

◊ Who will you reach out to at your moment of struggle? Write their name down.

· Which style do you fall into most easily: self-directing, deferring, or collaborative? What might it look like to see yourself as working together with God?

8

married sex: can it be good?

> She noticed that the window, the bedroom window, was open.
> ... How exactly like Mark! Obviously it was high time she
> went in.
>
> C. S. Lewis, That Hideous Strength, *The Space Trilogy*

Maurice and Monica weren't sure their marriage would make it.
They had lived together for a few years prior to getting married,
but when they became Christians, they knew getting married was
the right thing to do. They started going to church and imagined
everything would now be okay. But their misery only increased.
Maurice was emotionally disengaged. Monica had an affair. Sex
was one of the few things they had in common but it was usually
make-up sex. That was better than no sex, but there was no real
intimacy between them. They wondered why they couldn't make
marriage work.

Both Maurice and Monica came with broken mental templates around relationships, marriage, sex, and intimacy. None
of the marriages in their families had lasted; all had been marred
by infidelity, violence, addiction, and/or divorce. None of their

long-term friends were married; all were either shacking up or hooking up. They had no internal mental map of what healthy intimacy in marriage looked like.

Stewart and Sophia weren't sure their marriage would make it either. Both sets of parents had been married fifty years and seemed to provide good role models. Stewart traveled a lot as a leader with significant responsibility in a Christian organization. He'd struggled with porn years ago but had successfully put that behind him. He felt blindsided when Sophia told him she was done with sex—for good. Now that the children were out of the house she started improving her physical appearance and hanging out with girlfriends, and she was reluctant to go to church with Stewart when he was in town. They, too, were experiencing no intimacy.

There are plenty of misconceptions or downright lies about Christian marriage and sex. Have you bought into any of these?

- If you don't have sex before marriage, God will bless you with a wonderful married sex life.
- If married sex is not good, it's because you're being punished for messing up sexually in the past.
- Sexual disconnection is frequent and normal at some point; you just have to learn to put up with it.
- The Bible gives you the right to demand sex as a spiritual obligation from your spouse. (1 Corinthians 7, anyone? We will address this later in the chapter.)
- If you're both Christians, good married sex should happen naturally.
- Christians shouldn't want or enjoy sex too much; it's worldly and ungodly.

- The goal of the Christian life is a happy sexually satisfying marriage and family.

Oh, you won't usually hear any of those lies said out loud, and some include just enough truth to give them plausibility. But listen to the subtext you pick up on Sunday mornings, in your small group, at marriage conferences, or from many Christian marriage resources. Marriage has become a kind of god to much of the Protestant church. And marriage makes a very poor god. Nothing temporary can withstand the weight of being a god. Marriage is God's idea and it's absolutely worth fighting for, fighting hard for! But it's not worthy of worship.

Yes, God invented marriage. And married sex. And He considered it good, very good. He intended marriage, including married sex, to be an earthly physical demonstration of the kind of intimacy and love He experiences within Himself and that He desires to have with His bride the Church and each of us personally.

> Marriage makes a very poor god.

As important as the question "How's your sex life?" may be to a married couple, a more important question is, "How's the intimacy between you?" There's plenty of married sex going on with no intimacy, as Maurice and Monica are experiencing. Intimacy must be present for married sex to be good. But intimacy is possible even if intercourse is not.

This chapter could be a book in itself, or several books. Our purpose here is not to tell you how to have a better married sex life, although this is likely to help your sex life. We have space only to address how your individual sexual stories impact married sex, and how experiencing Jesus transforming your sexual stories can empower you to write new chapters of intimacy in your marriage.

I wish I didn't have to mention this, but I do. Some marriages are toxic. Not every marriage can be saved, but that's not because of any limitation on God's part. He can only do His full work in bringing a marriage to what He desires for you when both people involved give Him opportunity to do so. You cannot vote for your spouse; you can only cast your own vote. If one person delights in causing the other pain, that's toxic. Domination and control are toxic. Please note: Unhappiness does not make a marriage toxic. We're talking about a marriage that is continuing to cause you deep harm. If that is your situation, God may be releasing you from your marriage. God does not require you to continue putting yourself in a position to be harmed.

So what is the chance that married sex can be as God intended—good, very good?

Learning about Married Sex

Your previous sexual story doesn't go away when you say "I do." Biology is real, and there are sexual differences between men and women physically and emotionally. *Viva la différence!* But your sexual story powerfully impacts whether you avoid married sex or want more of it, and the kind of sex you pursue (or don't).

Before getting married I knew my internal expectations around sex were not whole. I'd invested much in my healing journey before God brought my husband into my life, but I knew I needed more. During the few months prior to getting married I marinated in the Song of Songs, the only book in the Bible wholly devoted to the uncensored relationship of a lover and his beloved, a relationship characterized by mutually fulfilling passionate sex and deep emotional intimacy. As a practicing ob-gyn physician and an ordained doctor of ministry, I knew more facts about sex than many people, but once I got married I soon realized there was a lot I still needed to learn. Intimacy is a whole lot more than left-brain knowledge, and I had to take coverings off my body, mind, and soul I hadn't even realized were there.

That's what it means to develop a one-flesh relationship.

What did you expect from married sex? Perhaps you expected it to just "work" since both of you saved yourselves for marriage. Or perhaps you wondered if you'd be able to "do it" after significant sexual harm in your past. You might have looked for married sex to be the same as what you had in other sexual relationships or a previous marriage. Maybe you hoped marriage would cure your porn problem. If you were sexually discipled by porn, that likely colored your expectations of your spouse's sexual responses and desires. If you'd been having sex with your partner before marriage, you might have felt confident sex would continue as good, or perhaps even better. You might have seen married sex as a necessary evil; God looks the other way, but you've got to "do it" if you're married.

There's a lot of truth in what I once heard someone say: "Before marriage the devil works overtime to get you sexually involved, and after marriage he works just as hard to keep you apart." You need to work together with God in pursuing intimacy. That starts with looking at the *you* that you brought into the marriage and how you are bringing yourself to the marriage now.

Your sexual story continues after the wedding. You married a sinner; there are no non-sinners available. And your spouse married a sinner too. You've hurt each other. You or your spouse may have betrayed your vows through having an affair, using porn, or other ways. And life happens. You've been disappointed, or perhaps traumatized, by married sex. These parts of your story all need to be brought into the light and offered to Jesus for Him to transform.

"I Hate Sex!"

Most of the time Jamilah could take sex or leave it. She would often avoid her husband's advances, going to bed before he did and pretending to be asleep. She might even pick a fight, perhaps unconsciously, knowing that would put him off for a time. Occasionally she could get into it, perhaps after a good date night or when he would sit and watch a movie with her. It would take her a while to get revved up, but she could enjoy sex once she did. Jamilah doesn't deeply hate sex, but she has a responsive sexual desire rather than a spontaneous sexual desire, and in that she's like many other people (more women but some men too). As she and her husband talk about sex, it's not that hard for them to imagine ways to make their sex life more enjoyable; they just need to be intentional about it.

Brianna truly hates sex. The very presence of her husband in the room makes her body tense and his touch makes her cringe. Her Christian upbringing taught her that if she didn't give her husband sex when he wanted it she would be his excuse to look for sex elsewhere, which he did. As her physical pain with sex increased over the years, she finally said, "No more." It's taking Brianna a long time to sort through her sexual story, but now she sees how her physical pain was, in part, her body's response to the masochistic and demeaning sex acts her husband had demanded. After many months, her soul is healing, and as she sees her husband also doing his heart work (with God and outside help), she's beginning to imagine what safety and closeness with him might look like. Sex? Well, we'll see.

Asexuality and sexual anorexia have become hot phrases in some circles today. I hate labels. Occasionally such descriptions can be a helpful shorthand but mostly they're hurtful. These labels put people in boxes marked "faulty" or "damaged." If you've been labeled this way, how does that make you feel? As you might do with an irritating label on the inside neck of a sweatshirt, cut off the label and throw it away. And then ask why. You didn't come to this place without a story. If physical pain, rejection, shame, abuse, or other harm has become connected with sex in your brain, it will take time to disentangle those mental pathways and build new ones.

When you think of having sex with your spouse, what messages or memories come to mind? Notice especially the thoughts that seem repetitive. Go there in your mind, and invite Jesus into that moment. Ask Him to show you His perspective. He will never shame or harm you. He's all about healing your heart so that pursuing intimacy with your spouse becomes possible.

If you're the spouse of someone who doesn't seem to like sex, get curious. Not in a twenty-questions kind of way, but seeking to understand. You will likely be tempted to take it personally, and there may be many things in your relationship that need addressing. But seek to understand your spouse's sexual story and look at the world through their eyes. Observe. Listen. Ask follow-up questions without demand. You might become an important catalyst for your spouse to experience safety and become more whole.

"I Need More Sex"

The number one question people ask online that brings them to our website is, "What do I do when my spouse doesn't want sex?"

Ebony wrote, "I thought men wanted sex. What's wrong with me that my husband isn't interested?" Alejandro wrote, "I don't just want sex. I want to be wanted by the person I adore more than anyone else in the world." If you're the one with the higher sexual desire, you can feel rejected, lonely, angry, or frustrated when your spouse turns away.

While these are generalizations, understanding some basic differences between men and women can sometimes help. On average, men see sex as the means to connection while women see sex as the result of feeling connected. Generally, men are more quickly aroused and satisfied while women commonly take longer to become aroused and may value the buildup of tension as much or more than orgasm. In about 75 percent of marriages the husband desires sex more frequently, but that leaves 25 percent where the wife has the higher sexual desire.

Let's tackle now what some people see as an elephant in the room: 1 Corinthians 7. The relevant core verses:

> But because of the temptation to sexual immorality, each man should have his own wife and each woman her own husband. The husband should give to his wife her conjugal rights, and likewise the wife to her husband. For the wife does not have authority over her own body, but the husband does. Likewise the husband does not have authority over his own body, but the wife does. Do not deprive one another, except perhaps by agreement for a limited time, that you may devote yourselves to prayer; but then come together again, so that Satan may not tempt you because of your lack of self-control.
>
> 1 Corinthians 7:2–5

Some religious leaders and (usually) husbands have weaponized this passage and used it to demand sex, sometimes demeaning sex, from (usually) wives.[1] But that's not the way of Jesus. Take the whole of the New Testament—there's no verse anywhere that gives anyone license to use Scripture to demand their "rights." Not one. Anytime anyone uses Scripture to demand their rights, they're wrong. Period. God has not promised you married life on your terms. Yes, God intends good sex to be part of marriage, but you are not *entitled* to anything, not even sex. Your spouse's no to sex does not provide an excuse to go to porn or masturbation. You can live fully alive without sex. (More on that in the next chapter.)

That said, married sex is truly important. But if you want married sex to be good, you will need to get over yourself long enough to realize the world does not revolve around you. In God's design you and your spouse are the most important people to each other. But if Adam looks to Eve to fill him up he will be sorely disappointed. If Eve looks to Adam as her everything, she will never become whole.

How does your sexual story connect with your desire for more sex with your spouse and your frustration when you don't get it? The lies and half-truths you believe, and the expectations you've brought into marriage, may have given you an unrealistic picture of married sex. Stop and consider:

- How has married sex differed from what you expected it would be?
- Has sex primarily been about getting your own needs met, and now that it's "legal" you *should* be able to get what you want?
- Has sex become the way you deal with unpleasant emotions?

- Have you come to see married sex as a "fix" for other problems in your relationship or as a way to fill up your empty soul in ways sex was never designed to?
- How has porn impacted the expectations you or your spouse have of married sex?

Some sexual integrity ministries have wonderfully served men and women, helping them stay away from porn, affairs, or similar behaviors. Hakeem has been a Christian for many years and dealt with his porn use through connecting with two such ministries. Now he's a small group leader for one of them, helping other men overcome addiction and live in sexual integrity. But his twenty-year marriage continues to deteriorate. He's not acting out sexually, but his wife says he's completely unable to connect with her. Hakeem has done good work on his outward behaviors, but has not dealt with the deeper matters in his heart. He doesn't yet understand the barriers he still experiences to true intimacy, or how to take the coverings off his heart in the presence of his wife so they both can see and know each other in the fullness of who they are as people.

Perhaps, like for Hakeem, Ebony, and Alejandro, something about sex and intimacy seems mixed up and unsatisfying in your relationship, for either yourself or your spouse. To sort that out you'll need to look beneath the surface and consider the *why* underlying the disconnect between you. This is not excusing bad behavior in either of you, but the more you can seek to understand the better you'll see what to do next in pursuing not just sex but intimacy. If you're a husband, seek your wife's heart before seeking her body. If you're a wife, let your husband be your hero.

And if your spouse wants more sex than you do, realize that may be because they truly desire connection with you. Do your own heart work to unpack how your story may have made sex less than good for you. Talk together about how your spouse could help you become aroused. Realize the important things sex does for your spouse, for you, and for the relationship between you. Take a mental step toward your spouse, and your body may well follow.

Sex through the Seasons of Life

You won't always be twenty. Or that might have been so long ago you can't remember what that felt like. Whatever stage of life you're in now, married sex can be good. The challenges are different, but the rewards of pursuing whole-person intimacy with your spouse are worth it.

Young newlywed sex may not be as magical as often expected. Your past sexual experiences may make it hard to fully embrace that you need feel no shame about sex with your spouse. Some, more often brides, struggle with going from no to yes. Cultural or religious messages may make it hard to now celebrate and enjoy your body and your spouse's body. Brain pathways from past trauma or previous sexual relationships can make it seem like someone else is in the room. Some husbands have a lot of performance anxiety. For the huge numbers of young people where porn has been part of their lives, married sex can seem so different from porn sex that your brain feels a bit of whiplash or deep disappointment. (That's another huge reason to stay away from porn.) Many people don't realize how common it is for women to experience physical pain with sex, and how seriously it dampens what you expected to be good.

Whether your honeymoon is your first sexual experience or not, it takes time to develop true intimacy and learn about each other's bodies and patterns of arousal. Some couples put so much effort into preparing for the wedding that they haven't done appropriate work to prepare for a marriage. The beginning of your marriage is building a foundation of intimacy that is designed to last for a lifetime. If you're young, it may seem difficult to think that far ahead. Talk about what you will do together to learn about sex and intimacy and intentionally nurture them. You might read a marriage book together each year and talk about it, go to a yearly marriage conference, connect with a couple in your church who can be marriage mentors, or invest in proactive marriage counseling. If issues such as pain with sex or difficulty with performance arise, get help right away.

Another season that presents challenges for married sex is midlife. Menopause is a time of major changes in a woman's biology which may lead to changes in sexual desire or arousal and often painful intercourse. Erectile dysfunction becomes a frequent challenge for men. You may both be busy in your careers, and your relationship has taken a back seat. If you are parents, the kids may now be leaving the house and the empty nest years stretch out in front of you. If your marriage has not been nurtured well, it may feel like, *Who is this I'm waking up next to? Do I even like you?*

Nobody ever taught you how to love well. But you can learn now.

As Stewart and Sophia from earlier in the chapter are experiencing, midlife often exposes areas where your marriage has not been maintained well. You may now feel you can't live with marriage misery any longer. In some ways that's not your fault; nobody ever taught you how to love well. But you can learn now. As you explore your sexual story and do the work to finish old chapters, it becomes possible to write new chapters with your spouse as well as in your own heart.

Almost all cases of painful sex at menopause can be helped with appropriate treatment. As a gynecologist, I've seen many women amazed at the difference small doses of natural estrogen applied vaginally can make in their experience of sex. If you are a husband with erectile dysfunction or similar problems, push past your embarrassment and get some medical assistance. And then do the work to invest in your relationship together.

Intimacy is worth fighting for even if penis-in-vagina intercourse becomes impossible. You can still make love to each other. Pleasuring each other's bodies, taking the clothes off your souls, two naked lovers coming together—that can continue regardless of age or medical condition.

Better Married Sex

Simone and Spencer were approaching their twenty-fifth anniversary, but their relationship was hanging by a thread. There had been no sex for a few years, and no intimacy for much longer. Spencer believed God doesn't condone divorce, so he was committed to staying, but he was miserable. Simone had been sexually molested as a teen and had never enjoyed sex. Both felt angry at God for not doing more to fix their misery. Neither was sensing His presence in their marriage. The kids were almost out of the house, and a future living as roommates seemed deplorable.

Simone felt embarrassed and powerless about her aversion to sex. She first embarked on coaching with me to get some insight on her troubled relationship with God. Periodically the topic of sex would come up; she'd dip her toe in the water and then pull back. It was months before she felt strong enough internally and safe enough with God to address her past experiences around sex and the walls between her and Spencer. Healing seemed slow.

God started dealing with Spencer too. He had to contend with his legalistic view of God and the entitled way he interacted with his wife and family. As Spencer dealt with the matters in his own heart, Simone noticed him becoming softer, safer, and more approachable.

Change comes through a process of transformation, sometimes in ways that seem quick, and sometimes in ways that seem very slow. Remember, two millimeters a day for brain change. After a long season of hard work Simone felt a breakthrough. She'd had moments with God before, but this was a big one. She'd looked at her sexual story enough that she recognized when God was doing something bigger, and this was it. Healing flooded her soul, her past lost its sting, and she now truly desired connection with Spencer.

She shared her experience with Spencer and his own heart work allowed him to respond with joy. A few days later they had sex for the first time in years. It was good—for both of them. And it wasn't just bodies coming together; their hearts were coming together as well. While it's not magical "happily ever after," they've both come to know God well enough that they can trust Him for their future without having to know all the details.

Can you experience better married sex even if things have been totally broken between you? Yes! At the risk of sounding cookie-cutter simplistic, here are five necessary steps:

1. Deal with your own stuff.

    Married sex will not get better by demanding more or different sex from your spouse. You can't change them; you can only work on you. What's it been like to be married to you? Would you want to experience intimacy with you? How safe are you? What baggage do you have yet to address? What walls do you have within your own heart? Have you learned to pursue intimacy with God that's more than left-brain facts? Has He been changing you from the inside out?

2. Talk about it.

Many spouses I talk to say, "I've told my spouse how much I need sex, and they don't care." Talking about it doesn't mean asking for sex; it means seeking to understand. It means taking the walls down around your heart and being vulnerable, listening not to rebut your spouse's perspective but to come closer together.

Talk about how you each learned about sex, what sex means to you, what helps or could help you each feel closer to each other, what arouses you, what you like or don't like about sex, what frightens or turns you off. You need to have the sex talk together regularly, along with developing rhythms of communication about all aspects of your relationship.

3. Make sex about the relationship, not about you.

Duty sex or obligation sex doesn't satisfy. God designed sex as a means to bond you closer together. As my friend Dr. Jennifer Degler says, "God knew that if we were to remain married for fifty years there would have to be drugs involved."[2] The neurochemicals released during mutual healthy married sex are like Velcro sticking you together.

Make sex a priority in your marriage equal to communication, practical working together, and prayer. Married sex is neither a god nor unimportant. Remember, it's not about *me*; it's about *us*. This means that if either of you believes having sex today would drive you farther apart, don't do it.

4. Be the invitation for your spouse to come closer.

How can you become the invitation for your spouse to come closer? This is not simply being nice. Sometimes it means having hard conversations so the barriers between you can be cleared away. It does mean you dispense with criticism, complaining, and manipulation. What would help your spouse want to come closer to you? Do that.

And then do it again, and again. Intimacy is like food: You don't eat once and then forget about it for a year. Keep being the invitation—today, tomorrow, and every day. Make it a lifestyle.

5. Invite God into your bedroom.

Good married sex was God's idea, and it's a key target of the enemy. In many ways this is bigger than you. What might it look like to invite God into the room as you make love to each other? Something exhilarating happens when the clothes come off your bodies, minds, and spirits in God's presence. Physical, emotional, and spiritual intimacy all at one moment. Not every sexual encounter will have the same intensity, but things will change if you invite the Inventor of sex to be present.

At least sometimes, pray together before making love. Ask God to bless your bodies, minds, and hearts and to be the glue holding you together. Thank Him for the gift of sex. Imagine Him sitting beside you as you pleasure each other, share your love, and once again become one flesh.

Can you see now how intimacy is not just two bodies taking off their clothes? True married intimacy requires two whole people being naked and unashamed. That's a life-long pursuit. Doing the work to deal with your past sexual story makes it possible to invite your spouse to see and know you, and for you to see and know your spouse. Physical, emotional, and spiritual intimacy all wrapped into one.

Pursue intimacy!

THREE'S NOT A CROWD

This intimacy stuff, it seems hard. Even scary at times. In many ways you'd rather hide. But the desire in your heart is harder than ever to dismiss. You've known moments that you might call intimate, and yet you long for more. That desire had been easier to ignore while handling the endless tasks of the day, but now that you're relaxed at home, the desire is all you're aware of.

When He's shown up in the past, it's been good, even if unnerving. But tonight your longing is for someone with skin on, your spouse. You can picture them right now—the look in their eyes, their voice, their touch, the smell of their body, the feel of their lips on yours. It's been a while, quite a long while.

A hundred thoughts race through your mind. Last time you felt this desire it didn't turn out well. A step toward them and your prickly spines came out. So did theirs. Your spouse pulled away. You pulled away. It was as if some invisible barbed wire between you mocked your desire and left you hurt, embarrassed, frustrated.

But since He's been showing up your soul feels different. The past isn't screaming at you the way it once did. You want to be seen, but you're still so unsure. Could he? Would she? Am I even able to? What if they . . . ?

The questions still fill your mind, but the sight of your spouse coming into the room triggers something even more from your heart. Part of you would like to run but something keeps you there. Your eyes meet. A few words pass between you. It's tentative. You're both checking each other's emotional temperature.

And you become aware that Someone else is there too. He's shown up once again. But now? What could He possibly want with you now? Is He here to squelch or divert your desire? Or could His presence perhaps make this chapter between you different—and better?

Your spouse also seems aware of Him, but the two of you can't keep your eyes off each other. You're seeing each other in a way you haven't in a long time, perhaps ever. Some of it's good, but you both also see the not-so-good parts of the other. And you keep looking anyway. Is this intimacy?

More words pass between you. You're not sure how long you talk, but you find yourselves moving toward each other. Your hands touch. Your lips touch. Body parts start getting entangled. Clothes start coming off.

Your brain is fully present with your spouse, but you also sense that He hasn't left the room—and that He's pleased. This is intimacy as He designed it, and His joy seems to sweeten the fullness you feel with more goodness than you could have ever hoped for.[3]

Questions to Discuss or Contemplate

- How have the sexual stories of both you and your spouse affected your relationship?
- What's been the sexual story of your marriage?
- How can you become the invitation for your spouse to come closer to you?
- How has the church, the body of Christ, helped your marriage? Has it made your marriage more difficult in any way?
- Imagine God being present when you and your spouse make love. How might that change things?

9

single, christian, and sexual

We often miss how radically countercultural it was for Jesus,
a thirty-year-old in first-century Israel, to remain single.

Christopher Yuan, Holy Sexuality and the Gospel

So, what's a single person supposed to do? If you listen to much of what's both said and unsaid in church, you get the message that, because God intended sex to be enjoyed between a husband and wife within covenant marriage, to be a good Christian you turn off your sexuality until you say "I do." And then if your marriage ends, you're supposed to turn it off again. And if you're not, can't, or don't want to get married, tough. Or maybe that idea is just old-fashioned and it doesn't matter what you do.

How's that working for you?

It hasn't worked for me. I lived single until God brought my husband into my life in my forties, and I'm living single again since he passed away. If you're not married right now, you'll probably agree with me that your nature as a sexual being and your need for intimacy don't correlate with your relationship status. I could rant about how the Christian church has, for the most part, utterly failed unmarried people. If you've heard any teaching at all, it's likely been, "If you're not married, just try harder and don't do it." There's been precious little help for those without a spouse to address their sexuality or their need for intimacy. But ranting isn't helpful. Instead of cursing the darkness, let's turn on the light.

In 2014 the *Washington Post* reported that for the first time there were more unmarried adults in the United States than married ones.[1] That trend continues both in the United States and in many other nations. Half of the Christians who were surveyed said they felt sex between unmarried consenting adults is either sometimes or always okay.[2] One of many statistics Christian sociologist David Ayers unpacks is that more than half of adult evangelicals have cohabited with someone not their spouse at least once.[3] There are certainly a lot of single sexual Christians out there. (By the way, "being sexual" does not necessarily equal "having sex.")

But you're not a statistic "out there." You're you, with your personal story and your own collection of emotions, shame, disgust, desires, vulnerabilities, needs, and experiences with others and with God. You might wonder, for example:

- What if I never find a spouse? How long am I supposed to wait? God knows I need sex; why isn't He bringing me someone?

- What kind of a God would withhold the highest joy possible from me—sex—just because I'm not married? I'm just not that spiritual.

- What if I don't want to get married?

- I may or may not get married someday, but in the meantime I like sex. I need sex. God doesn't really see it as that big a deal, does He?

- What if I'm only attracted to someone of the same gender? Am I supposed to never, ever experience sex, or sex again?[4]
- I've had sex before. My sexuality has been awakened. Even if I might have been able to go without sex before that's utterly impossible now; I know what it's like.

Did you notice anything the above questions have in common? They make some assumptions, including,

- I'm a sexual being, married or not. (This one is absolutely true!)
- Having sex with someone will fulfill my needs in a way nothing else can. (Really? Let's explore that.)
- God doesn't want me to have sex with someone not my spouse. (Okay. But is this what He cares about most?)

Follow those assumptions to their logical conclusions and you might end up believing God is an ogre. You either try hard and fall in line or you're bad, dirty, one of "those people." There must be more to the story. We're contending in this book that sex is never just sex. Behaviors are important, but what's underneath, the matters of the heart, are at least as important. Addressing these matters of the heart doesn't mean you can do whatever you wish without consequences. But stuffing facts or laws into your left brain is not effective at bringing you wholeness.

Salome is struggling to work through what following Jesus means for her sex life. She's living with her boyfriend and sex is good for the most part. They've talked of marriage, but he's not interested. Is she supposed to move out? Could she emotionally handle being on her own? Should she keep living with him, hoping he'll come around? She's ambivalent about giving God the vote in those questions, and unsure about what to do next.

Quinn's marriage ended a few years ago and he misses having someone to do life with. He has a strong sex drive and knows he could find a woman to have sex with any time he wants. But he hasn't. He wonders if he'll ever get married again: "Any woman my age will have baggage. Do I want that? What baggage am I willing to live with?" Although not having sex as a single middle-aged male seems very uncool, it's the other relationship issues that feel more problematic. If not marriage, does that mean he's destined to always feel disconnected and lonely?

So here's to addressing these matters of the heart for those of us who are single, Christian—and sexual.

Single and Fully Alive

In the opening of this book, I told you of how I found myself alone in a hotel room with a married man. One thing that experience pushed me to deal with was the lies I had come to believe. Our culture has promulgated the idea that in order to be a fully alive, whole human being you must have a satisfying sex life. The modern church has often extended that to the (often unstated) belief that to be fully alive you must therefore get married.

Really? Does that mean I wasn't fully alive until I got married in my forties? Have I slipped in status now that I'm single again? Are you somehow a second-class human being, or at least a second-class Christian, because you're not wearing a wedding ring? Should you make it your goal to get married? I've had so many people ask me, "Are you getting married again?" (For the record, I'm not looking.)

In the first fifteen hundred years of the church, being a single, celibate Christian was viewed as the highest, most spiritual life. The Protestant Reformation changed that, and for the last five hundred years the married Christian life has usually been held up as the pinnacle of success. Paul did not believe that either of these views were "the answer" spiritually. Right in the middle of his discussion of marriage and singleness he says, "Only let each person lead the life that the Lord has assigned to him, and to which God has called him" (1 Corinthians 7:17).

Rachel commented on our website, "Singleness is viewed as shameful and wicked. There's no doubt in my mind that the only real members of Christ's body are the marrieds. We [singles] are not truly part of Christ's Bride. I've been repeatedly told, 'Only married people can appreciate Christ's love for His Church.' I sure don't feel loved by Christ or His Bride." Part of me wants to weep with Rachel because I've felt that message oozing out of many churches and their leaders. And part of me wants to grab some Christians by the shoulder and yell, "Wake up!"

This is not a book advocating for either singleness or marriage—we're addressing the matters of the heart. And for many singles the desire for sex becomes shorthand for the desire for intimacy. Your sex drive may be very real, but like Quinn you may also be more troubled by the assumption that not having sex means not experiencing intimacy. What are you really hungry for when you want sex? And whether you desire sex or not, you absolutely must have intimacy in order to thrive.

Looking to Jesus is always the ideal way to go. And Jesus was never married, never had sex. Would Jesus have been more fully alive, more fully human, more fulfilled, if He had gotten married or had sex? Certainly not. If Jesus was fully human, as we believe, He had all the sex hormones, sex organs, and sex drives that any of us humans have. How did He make it? How did He deal with His sexuality?

I was talking about this very point with a group of men and women going through our Sexpectations course. One twenty-something single young man I'll call Dan said, "But Jesus was a special case. He was without sin, unlike the rest of us. Jesus was extremely tight with His heavenly Father."

Bingo! Dan was assuming that Jesus' example didn't really apply to him. But his response was truer than he first realized. What did Jesus know that we don't, but need to learn? Jesus wasn't encumbered by the belief that the spirit is good and the body is bad. There was no split between His body, mind, and soul; they were completely integrated. His whole being, including His body, was daily, intimately connected with His Father.

You come to submit your sexuality to your heavenly Father every day just as Jesus did.

That's a huge clue for those of us singles who are wrestling with our sexuality. Your sexuality is not something to be either hated or made into a god. Wholeness means your sexuality, as well as every other part of you, is welcomed into the full picture of who you are becoming. And that whole integrated you is undergoing ongoing transformation, becoming the beautiful thing God and you are cooperatively working toward together. You come to submit your sexuality to your heavenly Father every day just as Jesus did. And in doing so, you experience true intimacy with God.

I remember when, a couple years before I was married, I first learned to know God as my Husband (Isaiah 54:5). Now that I'm single again, that ongoing experience has become an important part of my life that I hold onto even more tightly than before. Your journey with God comes to the place where you truly feel seen and known by Him. He's the one filling your deepest heart needs, available 24/7/365. You're doing life with Him.

That may sound too . . . mystical. In the real world you're coming home to an empty apartment every night. Your sex hormones go on a rampage with some frequency. Your body is in the here and now, and it wants what it wants. And would anyone know or care if you didn't wake up tomorrow? As I once heard a six-year-old girl say, "I need God with skin on." There's no way intimacy with God can ever feel like kissing or holding your lover, or satisfying sex.

Here's something you may be surprised by: There's a sense in which intimacy with God wasn't by itself enough for Jesus either. A moment-by-moment connection with His heavenly Father was the air Jesus breathed, and He also needed people. He describes the connection you and I are to have with Him as intimate. "I am the vine; you are the branches. Whoever abides in me and I in him, he it is that bears much fruit, for apart from me you can do nothing" (John 15:5). You can't live, let alone thrive, for a moment without that connection. Intimacy with God needs to become the air in which you breathe also. And as human beings, we also need, truly need, intimacy with other humans.

Jesus, in His human nature, needed people. He pursued intimacy with people even at the risk of getting hurt. And He did get hurt! It was messy. His bids for connection weren't always reciprocated. He was betrayed by one of His close friends. One of His three most intimate friends denied Him. He was let down by those He relied on right when He needed them most.

And Jesus still pursued intimacy with people. A few people.

If Jesus needed that, do you think you can get by without doing the same?

Friends, this is not easy. I struggle with it myself. I'm naturally an introvert. My default is to hole up in my house curled up with a book. And there are times for that. But I've discovered that I truly need people. It takes significant intentional energy for me to pursue authentic intimacy with a few others, but it's truly worth it.

Now let's get practical about dealing with your sex drive as a single, and about what intimacy with God and with others is really like.

Handling Your Sex Drive

If you're unmarried and not thinking much about sex, you're not weird. There's nothing wrong with you. I would simply encourage you to be sure you have engaged your sexual story and invited Jesus into it. (Even if you're not thinking about sex, you still have a sexual story.)

But you might be reading this because you are thinking about sex a lot, and you're struggling with how to steward your sexuality in God-honoring ways. I get asked a lot of questions about handling your sex drive as a single Christian. Your sex drive is not something to despise; it's something to lead and guide rather than be controlled by. That's what it means to steward your sexuality.

We recently received this comment on our website:

I stopped watching porn years ago but could never stop masturbating. I found Christ last year, but I still cannot stop masturbating. Each time I feel masses of guilt and I repent again. Having sex/masturbating before finding Christ and then expecting to not have sex and or masturbate outside of marriage is the hardest thing I've ever struggled with as a Christian. I have made myself believe that anytime something bad happens to me it's a result of this sin.

Yolanda is engaged to be married and can hardly wait to have sex. She easily gets sexually aroused, sometimes listens to porn videos (just the sound), and finds herself masturbating. She feels embarrassed and ashamed. "I'm scared and wonder if I shouldn't [wait to] get married until I overcome this. I don't want to bring this into my marriage."

Peter is in his fifties, has never had a girlfriend, and wonders if not masturbating (not ejaculating) will predispose him to prostate cancer.

Carole is going through menopause, divorced, and every couple of months masturbates to relieve what feels like an enormous buildup of hormonal tension.

Yes, the M word. When I'm asked about masturbation, my response isn't as black and white as most people would like. We'd love a yes-no, right-or-wrong answer: Masturbation is either sin or it's not sin. I've received very specific—and differing—reactions from early readers, including pastors, about this section of this book. Just to be clear, the sentiments I express here are entirely my own. Scripture does not speak specifically about masturbation, and we must be cautious about making a definitive statement about something when Scripture doesn't. And in this book we're looking beyond the behaviors and dealing with matters of the heart, remember? What are the matters of the heart at play with masturbation?

> **What are the matters of the heart at play with masturbation?**

Not all masturbation is the same. On one end is frequent and compulsive masturbation that is controlling your life, accompanied by lust, sexual fantasies, or porn. You go to it for relief from frustration, boredom, sadness, or anger, and you celebrate with it when something good happens. You masturbate because you can't sleep, you have cramps, or you don't have a spouse and you feel horny. That's different from very occasional masturbation as a purely physical release of tension. I don't believe God looks at all these things the same.

Someone needs to be released from shame right here. I've encountered too many women who have heard the "masturbation is sin" message as an enormous blanket of shame over simple touching of their own body. I will not tell you specifically where the sin line is here, except to say that it's a matter of the heart. However, God does not drive you with shame.

And lust is always wrong. If the Holy Spirit is putting His finger on this part of your heart and saying, "This is something we must deal with," listen to Him. I can assure you there is no medical necessity for an orgasm. Your life will not be shortened if you don't sexually release. "Blue balls," or arousal without release, may be uncomfortable but will not harm you. I'm in no way minimizing your distress, just assuaging your possible concerns (or excuses?).

Masturbation is not an appropriate way to deal with lust or to express your sexuality. And there is absolutely no place for pornography of any kind for a follower of Jesus. A pastor friend told me a man cannot masturbate without porn. I can't speak to whether that's always true for all men. Many women I talk with say they do not need visual stimulation to masturbate, but they may indulge in sexual fantasies.

I told you this wasn't as cut-and-dried a conversation as you might wish.

So what do you do with your sex drive as a single? You do need a plan for when your sex drive is raging and you feel tempted to act out in whatever way you are tempted to by the brain pathways of your brand of sexual brokenness. In chapter 7 we talked about creating your escape plan. If you haven't done that already, do it now. If the plan you have isn't working, update it now. Make your plan practical. What you *do* with your body and your mind at those moments will make a difference. An escape plan is the first of three recommendations I give to anyone struggling with sexually acting out.

The other two things I regularly recommend are pursuing intimacy with others and intimacy with God. How do you do that as a single?

Intimacy with Others

Dr. Christopher Yuan is a professor at Moody Bible Institute. He lived a gay lifestyle before God got ahold of him, and now lives celibate while speaking, writing, and teaching about the gospel and sexuality. He writes about our need for intimacy as human beings regardless of relationship status.

> The New Testament has already created a new community through which our primary needs for companionship and intimacy can be met. Yet the problem is that we really aren't living as family. We aren't living as true spiritual brothers and sisters in Christ, and as a result, many singles—particularly those with same-sex attractions—experience feelings of confinement and isolation. . . . Spiritual family means that if the church were actually the church, if the body of Christ were actually the body of Christ, if the family of God were actually the family of God, then *not* having a physical family wouldn't really matter! Because we'd have *real* family. A family that is eternal.[5]

Those feelings of confinement and isolation are common among Christian singles regardless of who they're sexually attracted to.

So are you experiencing intimacy within the family of God? Do you feel like there are two, three, four Christian brothers or sisters who truly know you? New Testament professor Joseph Hellerman describes how in the ancient Mediterranean world the sibling relationship was seen as the closest and most affectionate bond, even above marriage.[6] That's the kind of connection the New Testament is talking about when it described the church as a family.

If you grew up with brothers or sisters, you know sibling relationships are messy. Sometimes you fight. It may be a love/hate relationship. If you've got several siblings, you feel closer to some than others. Sometimes you get enmeshed in unhealthy ways. Sometimes you become estranged or angry and don't speak for long periods. But your siblings are your siblings; you can't divorce your brother or sister. You may have never had siblings, or have never developed any real bond with the siblings you do have. There may have been so much trauma between you that you have set up necessary boundaries between you just to stay safe. Most of us need to learn healthier ways to relate to our siblings, but you're stuck with the siblings you have.

The family of God is messy too. But the only way to address our God-given need for intimacy is to stick around, as Jesus did with His closest friends. Who are your Peter, James, and John?

When I tell people my three recommendations—develop an escape plan, connect with others, connect with God—the "others" one is almost always the hardest. I've heard all the excuses. I don't have any friends. The people I know aren't safe. The people at church look down on me. I've tried to be real with my church family and it was horrible. The people I've tried to connect with end up stabbing me in the back. Everyone is absorbed in their own lives.

You still need intimacy, just like Jesus did, even if it's messy and hard. I've never met anyone who struggled with a significant sexual or personal issue who experienced long-term transformation and wholeness without connecting deeply with a few others. In chapter 5 we talked about some ways to connect with others. This is important regardless of relationship status, but especially if you're single. If you want to know where to put your energy in working together with God toward wholeness, work hard at finding a few of your people. And when you get hurt, pause for a moment, regroup, and pursue it again.

Getting this close to a few other people also uncovers the prickly places in your own soul that need further transformation. These are people who will call you on your "stuff," and you do the same for them. They will challenge you, and you will challenge them. But you stick around, and they do too. That's how you grow.

A word about physical touch for single people. Being skin hungry is real. Since my husband died I've become even more alert to this in myself and others. Sometimes when I offer a hug to another woman I just stand there and hold her until her body relaxes. Many women melt in my arms. Hugs from men are important too; my soul feels especially nourished when I get a lingering hug from one of my stepsons. I've heard from men that they have a similar need for physical touch. This can be slippery—it is not sexual! Be alert to the vulnerabilities in your own soul that tell you when something might become sexual. But also know that needing touch is a human thing. Jesus needed physical touch. Ask for and offer physical touch with others who are safe.

Knowing God As Your Spouse

This is not weird; this is biblical. "For your Maker is your husband, the LORD of hosts is his name; and the Holy One of Israel is your Redeemer, the God of the whole earth he is called" (Isaiah 54:5). It's a dimension of intimacy with God that all people need regardless of relationship status, but it's perhaps especially important for singles.

The reflections at the end of each chapter in this book have demonstrated some elements of knowing God intimately, and hopefully you've begun to experience a deeper level of intimacy with Him than you've known previously. Here are a few ideas to flesh that out even more.

Bring your body into your time with God. If you have five minutes, take the first minute or two to just be still, feel your breathing, and relax your body. If you have longer, make sure your body is present. Involve your senses: a candle, fragrance, music that draws you in, a comfortable chair, even a good cup of coffee. Time with God outdoors can be powerful. Feel the wind. Touch a tree. Listen to the birds. Look up at the stars. These days I often find myself walking or pacing in a relaxed way when I pray; moving my body seems to help. Your physical senses can be part of actually experiencing His presence.

Bring your emotions into your time with God as well. Whatever you're feeling, feel it in His presence. That's intimacy. Angry? Sad? Lonely? Worried? Excited? Express that to Him. Cry, yell, scream, throw rocks if you need to. You're bringing your messy emotions to Him; that's what you do with them. That's what God's very best friends in Scripture did—just read the Psalms. You intellectually know He sees you, but now you're experiencing Him seeing you. You're taking the walls down around your heart in His presence.

If you're scared to do so, you tell Him that too. And then get quiet. Just be still, *be* with Him. In our distracted culture it takes practice to learn to be still.

And then begin practicing the presence of God. Set reminders on your phone for two or three times during the day when you simply pause for a moment; "God, I'm here to connect with You again right now." The One Minute Pause app from author John Eldredge is one helpful way to do this. You're doing life with God. He's involved in everything, including your time, money, entertainment, work, friends, plans—and your sexuality. He's part of your good times, hard times, ugly times. You're not holding anything back. As David wrote in Psalm 139, you sense Him seeing and knowing you.

Inviting Him in, allowing Him in, will take practice. When you try to do this, you'll discover how distraction, fear, or the stuff of life constantly pulls you away from recognizing His presence. You struggle to see, feel, or hear Him. At times He seems to be playing hide-and-seek and you hate it, or Him. There are times when you are not sure you even want Him that close.

But keep taking the walls down around your heart with Him. Like Peter when Jesus asked him, "Do you want to go away as well?" reply "Lord, to whom shall [I] go?" (John 6:68).

Keep coming back. Keep saying yes.

SOMEONE TO COME HOME TO

You sigh as your hand pauses on the doorknob. You're coming home alone, again. The day's been full and your head's been full on the drive home. It doesn't matter whether the day's been good or bad, every evening is the same. What will you do tonight? Pour yourself a drink? Binge on Netflix?

A relationship would be nice, even if messy. This coming home alone is getting really old. It's no wonder you sometimes find any excuse to do anything but come home.

But as you open the door something feels different. The room feels somehow warmer and brighter than usual even before you turn on the light, as if someone had lit a fire in the fireplace. Have you walked into someone else's home by mistake?

You soon realize you're not alone. He's been here, waiting for you. His eyes twinkling, He moves toward you with a smile, and then pauses. You hesitate only a moment. The bags you were carrying fall to the floor and you take a step toward Him, falling into His outstretched arms. He doesn't let go, holding you until your body calms.

This certainly won't be your usual evening alone. He's here to spend it with you. He asks about your day and seems truly interested. His questions give you a different perspective on all that happened. He's started dinner and invites you to join Him in finishing preparation. As you sit down together to eat, your heart feels both fully present and overcome with amazement.

He joins you in working on a project for work. The significance of it seems quite different with Him here, and things seem to just flow. You've rarely if ever felt this much clarity.

The conversation moves to the future. You hadn't realized how tense and anxious you are about what's coming. He listens patiently as you share what's been worrying you. Just talking about it makes you feel less anxious. You ask Him questions. You hoped He would give you direct answers or an outline of tasks you should do. But that's not how He responds.

Just follow Me.

As you let His response settle in your soul, you realize it changes everything. You don't have to wrestle hard to figure things out and make things happen. You're not the one out in front fighting the battles alone internally and externally. He goes in front; all you have to do is follow.

You lose track of time as the evening winds down. How different the world, the future, looks than it did when you first opened the door. And His words keep echoing in your soul: *Just follow Me.*[7]

Questions to Discuss or Contemplate

- If you're single, what has been the most frustrating part of your relationship with God? With the body of Christ, the church?
- If you're discussing this with others, talk about your escape plan. Your escape plan might help them, and you can learn from theirs also. How might your escape plan need to be updated?
- What are you afraid of as you think about finding a few of "your people" to connect with often and deeply?
- How might you change your personal time with God so that your body, emotions, and heart are more present?

10

the ultimate story: intimacy forever

Man's chief end is to glorify God, and to enjoy him forever.

Westminster Shorter Catechism

Don't you love a good love story? A good adventure story? All the really good story lines have both love and adventure built into them. The questions keep us hooked. Will the hero get the girl? Does he have what it takes to make it? Will she recognize her hero, her true love? Will she know how much he loves her? Or will she give her heart to the deceptive but often charming villain? The hero must often wage war against the world, the flesh, and the devil to prove his love to her, win her heart, and rescue her from death or some fate even worse.

It's her heart he's really after. And she wants to give her heart away, to someone who is truly worthy. These may sound like chick flick ideas. Hey, I'm a woman, so this language may come easier to me, but the need and desire for intimacy is not gender specific. "I want my wife to want me," wrote Paul. "How can I give myself to my wife if she is only giving part of her heart to me?" mused Jeremy. John, who leads a recovery group of men working toward sexual wholeness and freedom from pornography, told me that the group's common, biggest struggle is feeling alone in this journey.

This need and desire for intimacy is the storyline of great movies such as *Casablanca*, *Romeo and Juliet*, *West Side Story*, *Shrek*, and *Pretty Woman*. It's the storyline of so many of the individual stories in the Bible, and the storyline of the book as a whole. Passionate covenant love "till death do us part." Spurned love, adultery, treachery, wounded hearts and souls. And then the Hero returns and regains the heart of His beloved. These stories are not about sex; they are about the cravings of the human heart for intimacy.

The way we are created for intimacy can lead to love. It can also lead to war. Evil has hijacked this need in ways that bring untold heartache, abuse, and even death. As we've explored together, the wounds in your soul when intimacy goes wrong are deep. In response you either close yourself off behind walls of self-protection, or rush headlong from one experience or relationship to another in a desperate attempt at connection.

Again, God created every human being, including you, with the need, desire, and capacity for intimacy. We've addressed your need and desire. We've talked about the kind of wholeness Jesus is inviting you into and some of the critical elements in that journey. We've addressed some ways to pursue intimacy regardless of your relationship status. Your past is losing its sting. In working together with God you've undone the lies you had come to believe, and the wounds you've experienced are being healed, but what about the remaining empty places in your soul? Can you ever be totally filled? In some sense you may be feeling relieved that you're coming back to a baseline, but is this as good as it gets? Have you been so marred that you can't ever hope to experience the ecstasy of *full and complete* intimacy? Does your heart still have the capacity to experience shalom, Eden, light with no darkness at all, true joy, like the characters in one of those love/adventure stories?

That's not a rhetorical question. The answer is simple—yes! This is not only for someone else; it's for you too.

A New Kind of Lifestyle

Our modern culture makes it challenging to look beyond the moment. We've become accustomed to microwave dinners, entertainment on demand, and instant gratification for almost any desire. We want a pill to instantly fix whatever ails us. But there's no intimacy pill. You can't order intimacy from Amazon Prime and have it delivered within hours.

What if the journey is as important as the destination? Intimacy is not like corn, which is ready for harvesting in 120 days or less. It's more like an oak tree, which takes decades to mature. It's not something that happens to you; it's a lifestyle you enter into and continue to pursue. Refuse to look at your unfilled need and desire for intimacy with contempt, or to settle for lesser lovers. Use any remaining emptiness to fuel your continued pursuit—not for sex but for intimacy. This applies to pursuing intimacy with others (including your spouse if you're married) and with God.

The very fact that you feel some still-unfulfilled desire means you have capacity for intimacy yet within you. That's part of the image of God that evil has tried to destroy and distort, but it still remains. Your capacity is the reason everything up to this point has not yet fully satisfied your soul.

Your need for intimacy won't be "fixed" just by reading this book. My desire for you is not that you read these chapters and now feel completely whole and filled. My words can't do that. What I hope and pray is that this book has cleared away some roadblocks on your journey to intimacy, that you are fanning the flame of hope that intimacy is possible for you, and that you are embarking on a lifestyle of stewarding your sexuality and pursuing intimacy for as long as you are here on earth, and also for eternity.

You now have important tools to do that. You've experienced how to invite Jesus into the hard parts of your sexual story, and you can do that again any time stuff from your past tries to sabotage your journey. You've learned some practical ways to pursue intimacy with others regardless of your relationship status. It's messy. It's hard. And you can do it anyway, just like Jesus did. You've experienced coming closer to Jesus, bringing your body, mind, and soul into His presence in the present, learning to be truly with Him.

We need to unpack three further important elements of your ongoing pursuit of a lifestyle of intimacy: vulnerability, being the invitation, and giving and receiving.

Vulnerability

Being vulnerable means being seen and known, letting the walls down around your heart. You feel exposed. You might get hurt. You have been hurt; that's why the walls have been up. Why would you want to take or leave them down? The truth is you've been hurt by people, and you will find your healing in connection with people. Deep, lasting connection with God is vital, but He doesn't bring you healing in a vacuum. He created you for connection with others. As C. S. Lewis wrote,

> To love at all is to be vulnerable. Love anything, and your heart
> will certainly be wrung and possibly be broken. If you want to

make sure of keeping it intact, you must give your heart to no one, not even to an animal. Wrap it carefully round with hobbies and little luxuries; avoid all entanglements; lock it up safe in the casket or coffin of your selfishness. But in that casket—safe, dark, motionless, airless—it will change. It will not be broken; it will become unbreakable, impenetrable, irredeemable. The alternative to tragedy, or at least to the risk of tragedy, is damnation. The only place outside Heaven where you can be perfectly safe from all the dangers and perturbations of love is Hell.[1]

Just this week I was talking with Amy about her past experiences of same-sex attraction and addiction to porn. She's now been successfully married to her husband for nearly twenty years. What changed things for her was not intellectual truth; she knew plenty of that. What changed for her was finding intimacy with Jesus. At first she was scared—would He reject her? Could she even say to Him the words that described what filled her with so much shame? She wrote a letter to Jesus, then turned on the hair dryer so she could barely hear herself read aloud what she'd written. As difficult as that was, being vulnerable with Jesus in that way started her journey of transformation.

I'm not sure we ever experience full and completely safe vulnerability here in this life. It's an ongoing journey of being seen and known, both with a few reasonably safe others and with God. And the process is worth it.

Be the Invitation

You can't demand intimacy. Oh, you might try. But that ends up in either abuse or superficial pretending.

There are deep ways in which intimacy and love are similar. Can we even tell the difference between them? Being deeply seen, heard, and known feels like love, and it is.

You can't command love. Again, you might try. You might get obedience or niceness as a result, but you won't get love. You can't give or receive love or intimacy on demand. Your heart needs to be won. And so does the heart of the person you're seeking to deeply connect with.

God set up love and intimacy such that not even He can demand it. God is continually inviting us to come closer, to let down our walls, to take the coverings off the various parts of our lives and hearts and be with Him. Jesus says, "Behold, I stand at the door and knock. If anyone hears my voice and opens the door, I will come in to him and eat with him, and he with me" (Revelation 3:20). We sometimes think of this as a one-time invitation. But the sense of the Greek is that He is *continually* standing and knocking. It's His constant posture toward us. He *is* the invitation.

> Don't see yourself as trying to find the right formula to convince someone to come closer; you **be** the invitation.

And we need to adopt that posture as well. I hear the common complaints: "My spouse won't talk to me." "I don't have any friends." "My spouse won't have sex." "The people I know don't like me." Don't see yourself as trying to find the right formula to convince someone to come closer—you *be* the invitation. None of us do this perfectly, but by adopting the mindset of invitation—embracing God's loving, consistent invitation to you and letting that invitation extend through you to others—you'll find others are much more open to taking a step in your direction. What's it like to come closer to you? Would *you* want to come closer to you? Try being the invitation.

That may seem hard. Your past or your personality may make it easy for you to withdraw, or you become desperate and grasping. Your shame seems like an ugly blanket you repeatedly struggle to get away from. But keep practicing. Notice what matters to your friend, your coworker, your spouse, the person at church or small group. Be curious and interested. Keep being the invitation. Not everyone you seek to connect with will respond, but some will. You'll find the empty places in your soul becoming less empty, and your capacity for intimacy will increase even more.

And remember how Jesus feels about you. "Whoever comes to me I will never cast out" (John 6:37). His invitation is constantly open to you to come closer. He is still the invitation even when you mess up, when you forget Him, when you internally imagine Him as distant, disinterested, or condescending. All the enemy's lies about Him that you've previously believed are just that—lies. Keep running *to* Him; His invitation to you is always open.

Giving and Receiving

Intimacy is a two-way street. Some people more naturally seek to get. They approach others looking to be filled up by them. We've talked about how that is a no-win scenario. Others may struggle to *take in* any goodness from others. My husband, Al, said several times, "I think I've been a pretty good giver in my life, but I haven't always been a good receiver." That struggle to receive may come from feeling you're not worthy of whatever goodness others might offer. "If they really knew me, they wouldn't want to be close to me." That impacts how you see God as well.

Pursuing intimacy pushes you past either of those one-sided views. For intimacy to work you have to learn how to consider others, to truly see them and seek to know them. You have to practice giving of yourself, being truly present. And you also have to let your own walls down, giving others a chance to see you and offer something to you. For some people that may be the harder aspect of intimacy. It can feel even more vulnerable.

There's something immensely satisfying about experiencing how the gift of your presence ministers to someone else, whether sexually with your spouse, or heart to heart with another person. When you step outside yourself enough to truly offer yourself, and the other receives you, you get filled up too. You, your presence, made a difference. That's both giving and receiving. And it never gets old.

Others cannot completely fill you up, heal you, or fight your battles for you, but they can minister to you. You'll feel a lot less empty if you choose to receive the things others can offer. It's imperfect, sure, but allow your soul to receive the kind words, presence, encouragement, support, or prayers others do provide. And if it helps you do so, remember that receiving something another person offers is truly a gift to them.

For Here and for Eternity

As good as this life on earth may get, it's never enough. It doesn't matter how many years you live, how much money or things or success you have or don't have. It doesn't even matter how many people you have around you. It's never enough. It never can be enough. Because we were created for more. We were created for eternity.

Two things are true. First, there is real, honest, and lasting healing, transformation, intimacy, and goodness here and now, in this life. Because of Jesus you don't have to stay where you are. Your journey to sexual wholeness can—must—continue even after you finish reading this book. You can have so much more than you've yet come to experience. Each of us taps only a small portion of all that is available to us here and now. The goodness we experience in this life is also accompanied by what the Bible calls tribulation,[2] but there is an exponentially bigger and more whole life available to each one, including you.

And the second truth is that this will never be enough. God designed it that way. He didn't create you to live a few years—or many years—in this world and then die. He created you for eternity, and some part of your heart knows it. "He has made everything beautiful in its time. Also, he has put eternity into man's heart" (Ecclesiastes 3:11). This is, in part, why the best marriage, the closest friendship, the experience of being seen and known by a few other humans will never leave you totally filled up. First of all, because you're leaky: Your soul begins to leak goodness the moment you receive it. And also because there are parts of you that will only be fully satisfied when you see Him face to face.

> We were created for more. We were created for eternity.

Theologians call this "the already and the not yet." The kingdom of God is here now, in reality. And the kingdom of God will come in fullness only in eternity, when Jesus returns to restore all things at the end of the age.[3] This is what Paul was talking about as he closes his famous love chapter: "For now we see in a mirror dimly, but then face to face. Now I know in part; then I shall know fully, even as I have been fully known" (1 Corinthians 13:12). There remains a dimension of fully knowing and being known, ultimate intimacy, that comes only in eternity. Christopher West relates this directly to our sexuality as "an invitation to the ultimate satisfaction of eros in an eternal communion beyond our wildest imaginings."[4]

God made us this way by design. He could have created a race of beings to tend planet earth and carry out His directions, but

He wanted more. He wanted a family. Adam and Eve knew God intimately, walking and talking with Him as openly and visibly as you talk with the people you care about. Evil came and disrupted all that, and God put in place the plan He always had in mind. God, in the Person of His Son Jesus, came to be Emmanuel, God with us.[5] This wasn't God speaking to us with some mysterious voice from on high, but coming to be flesh and blood with us. John talks about "That . . . which we have heard, which we have seen with our eyes, which we looked upon and have touched with our hands" (1 John 1:1).

And God won't stop until His dream has been accomplished.

And I heard a loud voice from the throne saying, "Behold, the dwelling place of God is with man. He will dwell with them, and they will be his people, and God himself will be with them as their God."

Revelation 21:3

He desires intimacy, intimacy with you, more deeply than you do. His need for intimacy is greater than yours as He is greater than you. And the amazing news is that He will make it happen! God's vision of the future is of you experiencing intimacy and fullness and satisfaction and joy beyond your wildest dreams.

Intimacy is the whole plan of redemption. Intimacy created, intimacy gone wrong, intimacy restored. No wonder the struggle is so hard. No wonder the longing in your soul won't go away.

Something this grand is worth pursuing for the rest of your life, regardless of the ups and downs. Continue dealing with your own stuff any time God brings it up so that you become increasingly capable of more and more intimacy. Let God continue His good work of restoring, healing, growing, transforming you from the inside out. Keep pursuing that intimacy with Him—live in it. Value, treasure, and pursue moments of real connection with others. Offer moments of real connection to those near you.

And keep your eyes on eternity, when God's desire for intimacy with you and your need, desire, and capacity for intimacy will be completely and eternally realized.

A THEOLOGY OF HOPE FOR TODAY

You're in one of your reflective moods. Your longing for intimacy is greater than ever, but questions keep running through your mind. Will your sexual behaviors lose their hold on you to the point you feel forever free? Will you be able to handle your sex drive long-term? Will you ever find a friend, a few friends, with whom you can experience seeing and being seen, knowing and being known? Will your marriage ever provide real intimacy? Will this intimacy with God continue to "hold" you when hard stuff happens?

You notice your ruminations are about tomorrow. You remember the times He showed up and dealt with your past. That was good; you're grateful. And you've experienced Him being with you in beautiful moments in the present. But will it last? Do you have what it takes to make it? You can't help thinking of all the times you've tried harder and failed. Will the future be any different? Is hoping for things to remain different anything more than an empty wish?

As the questions run through your mind, suddenly He is here again. It's always good when He shows up, even if unpredictable. You're not anxious about His presence in the way you were when this journey began. He's still so much more than you are, more than you can put into words. But He's also so real, so present, so with you and for you.

His eyes, as always, are an invitation. You've come to know He's safe, even if He never leaves you the way He found you. You begin speaking all the questions in your mind. If this has all been a short-lived experience and you'll just end up alone again, back where you were in all your mess, then it's been a cruel joke. You don't really imagine He'd do that, but you feel so shaky. The healing changes in your heart feel so new and tenuous. Is this really real?

He's not put off by your questions. And then it's as if you gain a new dimension of sight. You see your future as a series of rooms, each room a day, one after another. The vision becomes very fuzzy as you look beyond the next few rooms/days, and for just a moment you feel a twinge of anxiety. But He's not fazed by it at all.

You see Him move through the door into the next room, the one labeled "tomorrow." Without a hint of surprise or un-easiness He looks around, checking out all the furnishings, the closets, the people, the timeline, the events, the hills and valleys. There's not one thing about tomorrow that He doesn't see, review, and orchestrate into His plan for your future.

And then He speaks. "I'm here in your tomorrow. You can come into tomorrow knowing I've already checked it out, and it's okay. There's nothing here that we can't handle together. And when you get here, I'll already be here waiting for you. I'll be checking out each of your tomorrows before you get there."

He reaches out His hand. You pause only a moment, then step toward Him, taking His hand. Together the two of you walk across the threshold into tomorrow.

You're not alone. You will make it. And you can choose to feel confident that the next chapter of your story—that the two of you will write together—will be a good one.

Questions to Discuss or Contemplate

- What is your favorite love/adventure story? What does that story tell you about the longings in your own heart?
- How does seeing the whole of the Bible—as God seeking and restoring intimacy with us—affect your view of the plan of salvation?
- What dimensions of intimacy do you sense God inviting you to pursue here and now in this life?
- How does your longing for eternity impact your pursuit of intimacy now?
- How can seeing Jesus already in your tomorrow affect any concerns you have about your future?

acknowledgments

God has a wonderful sense of humor. I think He chuckles at the irony of having me write a book such as this, me who had higher and thicker walls up around my body, mind, and soul than anyone else I've personally come to know.

I'm grateful first to those people God used as part of my own becoming. Will Alexander, Dr. Marion Mosely, and other professional helpers were instrumental in the dismantling of my own walls so that I could become capable of experiencing intimacy. I also thank those professors at Oral Roberts University who were most involved in my professional development, especially Dr. Thomson Mathew, Dr. Bill Buker, and Dr. Ed Decker.

The idea for this book would never have come to be without the input, insight, and encouragement of my team, including Woodley Auguste, Omar and Madeline Galarza, and Kristin Sharrow. Priceless also has been the response from coaching clients, website readers, email corresponders, and podcast listeners who have trusted me with their stories, sometimes in small parts and sometimes in great detail. While no story in this book is from one single such individual, your stories have shaped me and more importantly, the content of this book.

The privilege of talking with so many guests on the *Relationship Prescriptions* podcast has shaped much of my thinking as well. At the risk of leaving out someone important, I'm especially indebted to Dr. Curt Thompson, Dr. Christopher Yuan, Dr. Juli Slattery, Laurie Krieg, Nick Stumbo, and Jonathan Daugherty for your expertise, your books, and our rich conversations.

Solomon said, "Of making many books there is no end" (Ecclesiastes 12:12). So why this book? David Sluka, acquisitions editor at Chosen Books, had to shepherd this book through the selection process, for which I'm overwhelmingly grateful. Jill Olson, my editor, has done much to make your reading experience a whole lot better than I could have ever done without her amazing expertise. You wouldn't be reading this without the efforts of Deirdre Close, marketing director, and her team. And none of this would have happened without Tim Beals, my literary agent. Thank you, Tim, for believing in me and in this book, and for walking me through countless landmines along the way.

Al Tanksley, while you'll never read these words you are present on every page of this book. When I was ready for human intimacy, God brought us together and I can't imagine my life without loving you. I was and truly am a blessed woman to have been cherished by you during our years together. I miss you every day and I can't wait to see you again in glory one day soon.

Most of all, I thank Jesus, for coming to earth as God *with* us, for creating me and each of us with the need, desire, and capacity for intimacy, and for entrusting me with this message. It's truly a high honor.

Finally, I thank you, dear reader. I pray for you even now, that Jesus minister His intimate, healing, transforming presence deeply to your soul, even as He did in mine. May you know the reality of true intimacy with Him and authentic intimacy with others in ways that nourish and fill your soul even while we all wait for the ultimate intimacy we will enjoy in eternity.

notes

Chapter 1 How Could This Happen?

1. From John 4:13–18, my paraphrase.
2. Judith K. Balswick and Jack O. Balswick. *Authentic Human Sexuality: An Integrated Christian Approach*, 2nd ed. (Downers Grove, IL: InterVarsity Press, 2008), 28.
3. Dan. B. Allender, *Healing the Wounded Heart: The Heartache of Sexual Abuse and the Hope of Transformation* (Grand Rapids: Baker Books, 2016), 22.
4. Adapted from Luke 19:2–5.

Chapter 2 The Sexual Story God Intended for You

1. Juli Slattery, *Rethinking Sexuality: God's Design and Why It Matters* (Colorado Springs: Multnomah, 2018), 36.
2. Curt Thompson, *Anatomy of the Soul: Surprising Connections between Neuroscience and Spiritual Practices That Can Transform Your Life and Relationships* (Carol Stream, IL: Tyndale Momentum, 2010), 15.
3. Dan B. Allender and Tremper Longman III, *God Loves Sex: An Honest Conversation about Sexual Desire and Holiness* (Grand Rapids: Baker Books, 2014), 1.
4. David T. Lamb, *God Behaving Badly: Is the God of the Old Testament Angry, Sexist and Racist?* exp. ed. (Downers Grove, IL: InterVarsity Press, 2021), 120.

Chapter 3 Intimacy Gone Wrong: How Sex Has Lost Its Glory

1. Curt Thompson, *The Soul of Shame: Retelling the Stories We Believe about Ourselves* (Downers Grove, IL: InterVarsity Press, 2015), 93.
2. Ted Bundy, interview by James Dobson, January 23, 1989, transcript, https://castimonia.org/wp-content/uploads/2013/01/ted-bundy-interview-transcript1.pdf.
3. Dr. Diane Langberg, "What God Hates: Abuse and the Church," March 22, 2021, in *Relationship Prescriptions with Dr. Carol*, hosted by Carol Peters-Tanksley, podcast, 24:09, https://drcarol.libsyn.com/what-god-hates-abuse-and-the-church.

4. Allender, *Healing the Wounded Heart*, 36.

5. If you or others have engaged in illegal activity, nothing here or elsewhere in this book is intended to imply that reporting to the appropriate authorities should be avoided. You may need to seek legal advice.

6. See Genesis 3:9.

7. See Genesis 3:11.

8. See Genesis 3:13.

Chapter 4 The Haunting: Where You Are Now

1. Christopher West. *Theology of the Body for Beginners: Rediscovering the Meaning of Life, Love, Sex, and Gender* (Erlanger, KY: The Dynamic Catholic Institute, 2004), 14.

2. See Luke 24:41–43; John 20:27.

3. See 1 Corinthians 15:53–54.

4. For a thoroughly gospel-centered neurobiological approach to this topic see Curt Thompson's book *The Anatomy of the Soul: Surprising Connections between Neuroscience and Spiritual Practices That Can Transform Your Life and Relationships* (Carol Stream, IL: Tyndale Momentum, 2007).

5. West, *Theology of the Body*, 63.

6. Jay Stringer, *Unwanted: How Sexual Brokenness Reveals Our Way to Healing* (Colorado Springs: NavPress, 2018), 118.

7. Adapted from John 4:10–26.

Chapter 5 Healing Is a Choice: Embracing the Process of Transformation

1. See Galatians 1:13; Philippians 3:13–14.

2. See John 4:15.

3. Love and Truth Network, loveandtruthnetwork.com.

4. Pure Desire Ministries, puredesire.org.

5. John Townsend, *People Fuel: Fill Your Tank for Life, Love, and Leadership* (Grand Rapids: Zondervan, 2019), 167–186.

6. Curt Thompson, *The Soul of Shame: Retelling the Stories We Believe about Ourselves* (Downers Grove, IL: InterVarsity Press, 2015), especially 145–149.

7. Celebrate Recovery home page, accessed November 25, 2022, https://celebraterecovery.com.

8. Edwin E. Abbot, *Flatland: A Romance of Many Dimensions*, first published in 1884.

9. See John 1:38.

10. See John 5:6.

11. See Revelation 3:20.

Chapter 6 Facing the Opposition

1. C. S. Lewis, *The Screwtape Letters* (New York: Macmillan, 1982), 3.

2. Carol Peters-Tanksley, "Decreasing Anxiety through Training in Spiritual Warfare" (DMin diss., Oral Roberts University, 2009), 134.

3. See Matthew 10:1; Mark 16:17; Luke 9:1; 10:19.

4. See Ephesians 6:10–14. Note how many times Paul uses the word "stand." This is not anxious striving; it's simply standing firm.

5. Christopher West, *Theology of the Body for Beginners: A Basic Introduction to Pope John Paul II's Sexual Revolution* (West Chester, PA: Ascension, 2004), 12, emphasis in original.

6. These paragraphs on the three clues to know you're under spiritual attack are condensed from Carol Peters-Tanksley, *Overcoming Fear and Anxiety through Spiritual Warfare* (Lake Mary, FL: Siloam, 2017), 157–161.

7. John Mark Comer, *Live No Lies: Recognize and Resist the Three Enemies That Sabotage Your Peace* (Colorado Springs: WaterBrook, 2021), 6.

8. See Mark 5:1–20.

9. See Mark 6:7; Luke 10:1.

Chapter 7 Toward Restoration: The Journey Home

1. Kenneth Pargament et al., "Religion and the Problem-Solving Process: Three Styles of Coping," *Journal for the Scientific Study of Religion* 27, no. 1 (1988), 90–104.

2. John Eldredge, *Wild at Heart: Discovering the Secret of a Man's Soul* (Nashville: Thomas Nelson, 2001), 171, emphasis in original.

3. I'm grateful to Laurie Krieg for this visual picture of forgiveness.

4. Adapted from John 8:2–11.

Chapter 8 Married Sex: Can It Be Good?

1. Withholding of married sex can also be used as a weapon to manipulate and control.

2. Quote from live talk given by Dr. Jennifer Degler October 15, 2022. More from Dr. Degler at jenniferdegler.com.

3. God celebrates your lovemaking: "Eat, friends, drink, and be drunk with love!" (Song of Songs 5:1).

Chapter 9 Single, Christian, and Sexual

1. Hunter Schwarz, "For the First Time, There Are More Single American Adults Than Married Ones, and Here's Where They Live," *Washington Post*, September 15, 2014, https://www.washingtonpost.com/blogs/govbeat/wp/2014/09/15/for-the-first-time-there-are-more-single-american-adults-than-married-ones-and-heres-where-they-live.

2. "Half of U.S. Christians Say Casual Sex between Consenting Adults Is Sometimes or Always Acceptable," Pew Research Center, August 31, 2020, https://www.pewresearch.org/fact-tank/2020/08/31/half-of-u-s-christians-say-casual-sex-between-consenting-adults-is-sometimes-or-always-acceptable.

3. David J. Ayers, *After the Revolution: Sex and the Single Evangelical* (Bellingham, WA: Lexham Press, 2022), 117.

4. This book does not directly address questions of same-sex marriage. I can suggest Preston Sprinkle's book *Does the Bible Support Same-Sex Marriage? 21 Conversations from a Historically Christian View* (Colorado Springs: David C. Cook, 2023).

5. Christopher Yuan, *Holy Sexuality and the Gospel: Sex, Desire, and Relationships Shaped by God's Grand Story* (Colorado Springs: Multnomah, 2018), 130, 137, emphasis in original.

6. Joseph H. Hellerman, *When the Church Was a Family: Recapturing Jesus' Vision for Authentic Christian Community* (Nashville: B&H, 2009), 37–38.

7. Adapted from John 21:4–19.

Chapter 10 The Ultimate Story: Intimacy Forever

1. C. S. Lewis, *The Four Loves* (New York: Harper Collins, 1960), 155–56.

2. See John 16:33; Acts 14:22; Revelation 7:14.

3. See Acts 3:21.

4. Christopher West, *Theology of the Body for Beginners: Rediscovering the Meaning of Life, Love, Sex, and Gender* (Erlanger, KY: The Dynamic Catholic Institute, 2004), 114.

5. See Matthew 1:23.

CAROL TANKSLEY, MD, DMIN,

is an author, speaker, personal coach, licensed ob-gyn physician, and ordained doctor of ministry. She brings both academic expertise and years of experience as a practitioner to helping people experience lasting transformation in every aspect of their lives and relationships so they can thrive in the way God intended.

Dr. Carol received her doctor of medicine degree from Loma Linda University, Loma Linda, California. While still practicing medicine, she obtained her doctor of ministry degree from Oral Roberts University, where she was dubbed "doctor of souls" by the seminary dean and "doctor-doctor" by her classmates.

She makes her home near Austin, Texas, where she enjoys being Grandma Carol to four wonderful grandchildren.

More from Dr. Carol:

Online courses, podcast, blog articles, and more:
DrCarolMinistries.com

Free 30-day email devotional series, and more:
YourSexpectations.com

 @DrCarolT   @DrCarolMinistries